Hungry, And You Fed Me
Homilies and Reflections for Cycle C

Hungry, And You Fed Me

HOMILIES AND REFLECTIONS FOR CYCLE C

EDITED BY DEACON JIM KNIPPER

Published by:
Clear Vision Publishing
Manalapan, New Jersey
2012

Published by Clear Vision Publishing, Inc.
301 Highway 9 South,
Manalapan, New Jersey 07726

ISBN 978-1-4675-4816-8

First Printing November, 2012

Cover & Interior Design by Doug Cordes
Illustrations by Brother Mickey O'Neill McGrath

Hungry, And You Fed Me is printed on 60# Glatfelter Natural and the
text is set in Fairfield and Scala Sans.

Printed in the United States of America

CONTRIBUTING AUTHORS

REV. WILLIAM J. BAUSCH

JOEL BLUNK

REV. DR. DAVID A DAVIS

MICHAEL DOYLE

REV. PAUL A. HOLMES

DEACON GREG KANDRA

DEACON JIM KNIPPER

MICHAEL LEACH

REV. JAMES MARTIN, S.J.

FR. RICHARD G. MALLOY, S.J.

REV. CAROL HOWARD MERRITT

REV. PENNY A. NASH

MSGR. WALTER E. NOLAN

RICHARD ROHR, O.F.M.

FRAN ROSSI SZPYLCZYN

The opinions in each homily/reflection do not necessarily represent
the views of the other contributors.

For my parents
Joseph P. Knipper (1929-2008)
&

Jean Sullivan Knipper (1927-2000),
who first opened my eyes to the wonder of our God

———————

And for all who hunger in mind, body and soul

"God writes the Gospel not in the Bible alone, but also on trees, and in the flowers and clouds and stars."

Martin Luther

"It is not that the Gospel has changed, it is that we have begun to understand it better. Those who have lived as long as I have...were enabled to compare different cultures and traditions, and know that the moment has come to discern the sign of the times, to seize the opportunity and look far ahead."

Pope John XXIII

"For I was hungry and you gave me food, I was thirsty and you gave me drink, a stranger and you welcomed me, naked and you clothed me, ill and you cared for me, in prison and you visited me...Amen, I say to you, whatever you did for one of these least brothers [and sisters] of mine, you did for me."

Matt 25:35-36, 40b

"Receive the Gospel of Christ,
whose herald you have become.
Believe what you read,
teach what you believe,
and practice what you teach."

*from the Rite of the
Roman Catholic
Diaconate Ordination*

CONTENTS

ORDINARY TIME

FEAST DAYS

FOREWORD

Who doesn't like a good story? Count Christians among those who do.

Christians are storytelling people. We're descendants of story-telling people on all sides of the family, from the ancient Hebrews to pagan converts. We're formed by stories, many of which are cautionary tales embedded in the narrative, poetry, psalms, and parables that comprise our Holy Scripture.

Storytelling is central to the practical understanding of our faith. Think about it: the very structure of our worship includes time to retell our stories. It also includes time to tell stories *about* those stories before we come to the table of the Lord.

Sometimes we listen and get the message right away. More often than not, we need to hear the same story again and again before meaning emerges. Even then, meaning morphs over time. What we once took as literal eventually transcends the mundane. Conversely, what we once dismissed—or blissfully embraced—as metaphor may become staggeringly real. Shallow soil. Multiplying fish. Mustard seeds. Pearls. Strangers healed. Storms calmed. Death vanquished.

Spiritual meaning and the practical value of our holy stories emerge as we grow in faith, as we engage in spiritual practice such as *lectio divina*, and also as the result of listening to (or reading) how others interpret scripture.

Hungry, And You Fed Me: Homilies and Reflections for Cycle C is a collection of stories about our stories crafted by superb storytellers. Here, we're invited to engage with scripture at a deeper level by people of abiding faith whose work and words are grounded in theological education and active ministry.

The authors herein are teachers inviting us to contemplate what these ancient stories have to do with contemporary life. They breathe new life into these familiar passages from scripture and inspire us to put into our faith into action—seeing God in all things, seeing Christ in one another, living the Gospel.

Homilists often talk about sermon preparation as "breaking open the Word," but really it's the Word that breaks us open and then holds the promise of making us whole. For the glory of God.

Meredith Gould, PhD

PREFACE

I have been fortunate throughout most of my life to enjoy the fruits of great homilists—whether it was growing up in Colts Neck and listening to Fr. Bill Bausch, or at the University of Scranton enjoying the wisdom of the Jesuits, or in my home parish having our pastor, Msgr. Walt Nolan warming the congregation with one of his many homiletic stories.

As a deacon in the Roman Catholic Diocese of Trenton, New Jersey, I'm passionate about great homilies. For those of us privileged to preach, homilies provide us a unique opportunity to break open the gospel message. Over the past decade, through various occasions and contacts, I've been blessed to encounter Christian clergy and laity who are gifted with the ability to spark transformation by touching people's lives through their homilies, sermons, and reflections.

A year ago I launched this project, leading me to eventually reach out to a dozen men and women who are some of the best of the best when it comes to breaking open the Word of God. My goal was to compile and edit a book that would feed the heart and souls of the readers and act as a vehicle to raise money to feed the hungry and homeless. My hope and prayer is that this book does both.

Under the moniker of Homilists for the Homeless, these writers and preachers have generously donated their material so that proceeds from this book can be given to the four charities selected for this volume. This first of three books begins with Cycle C of the Lectionary for Mass, which starts the First Sunday of Advent 2012 (and every three years thereafter).

As Christians we are called to use the gifts that God has given each of us. Called to spread the good news of Christ. Called to reach out to those who live on the margins. Called to clothe the naked, shelter the home-less, and feed the hungry.

May these gifted words do exactly that and bring blessings to you and yours,

Jim Knipper
21 September 2012
Feast of St. Matthew, the evangelist

ADVENT SEASON

1ST SUNDAY IN ADVENT

DAVID A. DAVIS

JER. 33:14-16
1 THES. 3:12-4:2
LUKE 21:25-28,
34-36

| *"Be vigilant at all times."*

One of my earliest memories of school days when I was a child comes from a morning in first or second grade when we had to prepare a Peterson's Writing Specimen—a half-sheet of white paper, wide-lined, the class writing a series of letters and words in cursive, using ballpoint pens. Our very best effort in penmanship would then be sent away to the Peterson people who would send back the best in the class for proper accolades. I worked very carefully and did the best I could, the best ever, and I came to the end and had to sign my name. Bottom right, last line, I signed "David...David" I had to start all over. I was crushed. The second paper wasn't as good. I had to rush. Truth is, that one half-sheet of paper was the best penmanship of my life. My handwriting has never been any better; in fact, it has continually, over 40-some years, only become worse. My elementary school handwriting do-over.

Look around the sanctuary this morning. It looks, it sounds, it *feels* like Advent. Wreaths. Purple. Banners. Hymns. Familiar biblical texts. Tree lighting in Palmer Square. Horse-drawn carriage rides around town. Crowds for shopping. The Salvation Army bell-ringer. Counting days until Christmas. Here we go again! Advent I. The First Sunday of Advent. The beginning of the new year when it comes to the church calendar: Advent. Christmas. Epiphany. Lent. Holy Week. Good Friday. Easter. Eastertide. Pentecost. Birth of Jesus. Life of Jesus. Death of Jesus. Resurrection.

Holy Spirit…and back again. Here we go again. Come, O Come Emmanuel! Come Thou Long Expected Jesus! Even so, Come Lord Jesus! Advent. One big do-over! A re-write for those in English class. A mulligan for the golfers. In Harry Potter, yet another book. In music, a reprise… the return to the first notes of the melody. It's Advent. Here we go…again.

But it doesn't get any better. I'm not talking about our singing, or the opportunities here at the church, or the artwork, or how we do our worship, or one year's theological theme compared to another, or how well we teach and include our children, or how we do in welcoming newcomers this time of year, or when it comes to lifting up mission and outreach opportunities and God's call to us to be the body of Christ in the world. None of that is what I mean when I say it doesn't get any better. You know what I mean—life, the world, the struggles, the suffering, the kingdom coming on earth as it is in heaven kind of thing. The big picture out there, maybe in here (in the heart)…it doesn't get any better. Advent and this do-over thing!!

Most every year when we get to this Sunday, this First Sunday of Advent, the gospel reading tells of the teaching of Jesus regarding the Coming of the Son of Man. As in this morning's reading from Luke. "They will see the Son of Man coming in a cloud with power and great glory…be alert at all times, praying that you may have the strength to escape all these things that will take place, and to stand before the Son of Man." Jesus and his Second Coming. You recognize that Advent theme. We've been here so many times before; celebrating again the birth of Jesus while looking in faith to his coming again! In betwixt and between, the already and the not yet. Must be Advent.

The Coming of the Son of Man. The Second Coming of Jesus. The reference to Christ's coming again on Advent I, it always comes with this apocalyptic flair. You heard it in the reading: "Signs in the sun, the moon, and the stars…distress among the nations, the roaring of the sea, fear and foreboding, the powers of the heavens will be shaken…don't let that day catch you unexpectedly like a trap. For it will come upon all who live on the face of the whole earth." And preachers and teachers go to great lengths to try to explain biblical, apocalyptic literature, and the parallels to the Book of Daniel and the Book of Revelation, and the history rooted in the destruction of the Temple and the fall of Jerusalem and the already and the not yet of biblical prophecy in the context of the unique genre of apocalyptic, complete with warnings against those who want to predict and sell books and go political and decide who gets to go and who is left behind. Preachers and teachers like me go to great lengths to try to explain apocalyptic literature in the Bible every year, every Advent, every time we go through this again. Every do-over.

When you stop and think about it, such apocalyptic consciousness is not just about biblical literature. Nor is it only in video games and fantasy novels. More than 6,000 American soldiers have been killed in Iraq and Afghanistan. More than 30,000 American men and women have been wounded. Civilian casualties in Iraq alone as a result of war and ongoing internal violence by some estimates exceeded 200,000. South Africa is a nation of 45 million people. In 2007 5.7 million were infected with HIV/AIDS. According to US Census statistics, 39.8 million people in 2008 lived in poverty. 14.1 million of those were children. 1 in 5 children in the United States live in poverty. Statistics of apocalyptic proportions. Words with apocalyptic connotations are everywhere. Words like rampage, surge, violence. Workplace, family, random violence, war on drugs, pandemic. And the genre and language of the apocalyptic has made a rousing debut in the healthcare debate coming from every side of the aisle. Preachers don't prime your apocalyptic imagination. The world already takes care of that.

It's never that far from home, either, far from life in here, I mean. Every time we gather as the Body of Christ, you know there is someone whose daily battle is beyond description, someone who is living a story of endurance and perseverance, a family who is pinning the needle in struggle, someone labeled a "surviving spouse." Every time we come here there are words from your life and mine that start to sound like this biblical literature—they start to sound apocalyptic: reduction in force, downsized, metastatic, Alzheimer's, credit crisis, hospice, long term care, chronic pain, rock bottom, despair. I guess what I am trying to say is that the longer I serve in pastoral ministry the less I think I have to explain the literature of apocalyptic. You already know; not because of movies or video games or the evening news or politics but because of life. Life out there and life in here. Life and how when Advent comes around, yeah—it doesn't seem to be getting any better.

When these things take place, Jesus said, when that's how it feels, when the Advent do-over just isn't working…right then, stand up and raise your head, because your redemption is drawing near. Your redemption. Your salvation. Your liberation. Your forgiveness. Your new life. Your resurrection hope. Your life forever in the kingdom of God. It is drawing near. God draws near. Jesus draws near. Not just because the calendar marches on, not just because we're on the clock, but because life happens. Not because we've come around to Advent again, but because once again we come to Advent with a certain fullness to life that demands and cries out for the very fullness of God.

Stand up. Raise your head. Your redemption is drawing near. God draws near. Jesus draws near. Not just then, now. Stand up. Raise your head, not just to see the horizon, but to experience his presence now. The difference between apocalyptic fantasy in film, a fascination with post-apocalyptic survival—the difference between all of that and the apocalyptic promise of God, is the tense, the timing, the real presence of Christ Jesus when life is happening now.

Real presence. Christ is present here, just as he promised. "I am here. This is my body broken for you. This is my blood shed for you." Forgiveness. Liberation. Salvation. Redemption. Take. Eat. Drink. Stand up. Raise your head. Jesus nears. The sacramental, apocalyptic promise of God.

If you were to gather all this literature of scripture together, all the apocalyptic writings of scripture, one collector's set, special edition, it would of course end with the Book of Revelation. And right at the end, before the benediction that concludes the Book of Revelation, right before "The grace of the Lord Jesus be with all the saints. Amen." Right there at the end, Revelation 22:20—"Come, Lord Jesus!" ("Even so, come Lord Jesus" in the King James.)

Come, Lord Jesus. It's not a victory shout. It's not a political slogan that paves the way for four more years. It's not a billboard or a movie trailor intended for an endtime scenario. It's a gut wrenching, heart felt plea. A prayer. Dare we say it, a demand! Come, Lord Jesus. A prayer for the Advent do-over, especially when it's not getting any better. Not getting any better—you know what I mean. Come Lord Jesus. It is not "come and finish this all up!" It is "come, now, quickly, come right now!"

"Prepare the way of the Lord."

When winter is in the offing, we're not prepared to pull out our mittens. When summer announces itself, we may be caught off-guard—last year's bathing suit can't possibly fit. Spring can take us by surprise, too, because we're in no mood to do spring cleaning. The closets are fine just the way they are.

Seasons make their demands. Even if we're not ready. Even if we'd prefer to just stay in the season we're in.

Because Lent is six or seven weeks, Easter doesn't get in the way too early. But Advent is only four weeks, and before we know it, it's over. The cheerful shadow of Christmas hangs all over it—the priests are wearing purple, but Santa's already in his red and whites at the mall. The Church says "Wait," but Bloomingdale's says, "Come and get it!" The Scriptures speak of John the Baptist, but we'd prefer to hear about Jesus, all wrapped up in swaddling clothes, lying in a manger.

Seasons make their demands, though.

And Advent says: "Wait." It says, "Prepare." It says, "Repent." It says, "Convert." Its patron saint isn't the Baby Jesus—it's John the Baptist. And today, he's in a prison, a wretched hole in the ground, waiting for Jesus to come to his rescue. Just like you and me, sometimes: sitting in a hole of pain, suffering, anxiety, or worse, waiting for Jesus to come to *our* rescue!

And Jesus says: Tell John that there's miracles for everybody else—but none for him. The blind are looking; the lame are leaping. But John's head will be sitting on a platter soon enough, served up by a dancing girl for the amusement of partygoers.

Seasons make their demands.

Let's not allow Advent to run *its* course without responding to its demands. Sure, we can ignore it if we want to. But we'll miss the chance to do what Advent demands: Give in, surrender, give up, and wait for the Lord to come to the rescue.

I promise you: He *will* come!

ZEPH. 3:14-18
PHIL. 4:4-7
LUKE 3:10-18

"Rejoice in the Lord always."

After years of notorious church scandal and corruption, during a time of great distrust of the church, a saint came along who would help change minds and hearts. This saint had a great desire to counter feelings of anger, suspicion, or a lack of trust, and replace them with a love of the Lord. If you were in Rome during the 16th century you might have spied him, standing in a piazza or on a corner. He might stand out because he was often wearing ridiculous clothing, and sometimes half of his beard was shaved off. It was in this way that St. Philip Neri helped to change the course of church history, and bring many souls to know Christ.

Neri is known for his extraordinary evangelizing, which was helped by his offbeat sense of humor. By joyfully reaching out as he did, St. Philip left a huge imprint upon the church and the world. This was accomplished by engagement and conversations. These conversations often began with distrust or curiosity. They would eventually turn to laughter, which became moments of conversion for many.

Introducing others to Christ came naturally to Neri, and in a joyful way. In fact he once remarked that, "A joyful heart is more easily made perfect than a downcast one."

Joy is our theme today, the Third Sunday of Advent, also known as Gaudete Sunday. Gaudete comes from Latin, and it means rejoice. It is in our rejoicing that our hearts are made more perfect as we prepare a place to welcome Jesus, our Emmanuel.

Prepare a place for the Lord? What place? And we are to prepare a place with joy? What joy? In our culture, the broader call of these weeks is to prepare for Christmas. We spin ourselves dizzy sending cards, cooking, shopping, and socializing. This day is a marker on the Advent path that directs us to the heart of our joy, reminding us to focus on the Lord.

Every year I vow to practice a quieter and calmer Advent. I like to think that I will achieve it, but I rarely do so. This year I am busy, but I have attempted to trim some of my activities, resulting in the creation of a bit of needed space. This is a mirror of our liturgical season, so that a place for the newborn Lord might be prepared in my heart. That tiny space is like a manger in my heart.

If we keep our preparation focused on our hearts, rather than on our tasks, and we can also be focused on joy, we might be able to access new places. Now the birth of Christ might be anticipated with the silent, patient, hopeful waiting of this season. This joy is to be had now, not postponed.

In the midst of this, I am aware that it is dangerously easy to make religious practice into a dry, somber act, one that is certainly not joyful. How can we joyfully prepare this barren place for new life?

Joyfulness is the core of the words of the prophet Zephaniah in the first reading, which tells us to shout for joy, sing joyfully. We hear the message to *"be glad and exult."* We are told not to be discouraged because God is in our midst. We have a mighty savior who wants to rejoice in gladness. God is in our midst, having removed all judgment against us. Suddenly

I imagine St. Philip, with half a beard and funny clothes, telling people about the promise of Christ!

In his letter to the Philippians, St. Paul repeats the same message—rejoice! As if he understood that we might be skeptical, or disbelieving, and as if he knew that we would lack joy, he repeats himself, "I shall say it again: rejoice!"

What don't we understand about this? The Lord is near, and the Lord offers us peace that is beyond our understanding. This is what is available to us through Christ—a kind of joy not known before. "A joyful heart is more easily made perfect than a downcast one." St. Philip reinterprets St. Paul, who said it first, using different words.

Why then, is this so hard to integrate into our lives? I ask myself this question. Although we make our way, we stumble along, trying to muster some joy, gratitude, and hope, recognizing that God is already in our midst. That God is healing, forgiving, loving, reconciling and is right here, right now.

I don't know about you, but here we are, less than two weeks before Christmas, and despite all of my words, I'm not there yet. Just what do I find in my midst? There is anxiety over shopping, money, incomplete work, and simply not being good enough for God. Yet it is God who is in my midst, who is in our midst bringing us that joy in great abundance. We are not asked to manufacture joy, we are asked to respond to it in kind.

So now what? That all sounds good, but what should we do? This is the question at the heart of Luke's Gospel for today, "*What then should we do?*" John the Baptist, the forerunner of the Lord, is drawing attention to himself by baptizing and preaching. Unlike St. Philip, who often used levity, John the Baptist is very serious. Make no mistake however; they have more than a few things in common.

People want something, but they do not know what to do, so they ask him. John minces no words. Give more. You have two tunics? Good, give one to someone else! If you have anything, share it. Even the despised tax collectors want to know what to do, and John is as clear with them; do not take more than you are supposed to take. Sounds easy enough, but that went against the standard of the time. Of course, we must stop to consider this; John is addressing us as well. Can we do this?

And how is this joyful? It is, if we stop confusing joy with happiness, and begin to understand the state of our hearts when they encounter Jesus. When we encounter and stay with Christ, we find the heart of joy. We come to discover that God is in our midst, and we are forgiven. This God in our midst, this God-with-us, has given deep peace. This God, our Emmanuel, has come to save us in the form of the Christ child. That is at the heart of our joy.

Perhaps then, out of that heart of joy, we can find the ability to both prepare a place for the Lord and also to give what we have away. We can do this because of one joyful fact: the more we come to know Christ and give everything away, the more he comes to live in our hearts. Now that is cause for rejoicing! And it is in that rejoicing in Christ that our hearts, perhaps not joyful at first, might be turned to him.

MIC. 5:1-4A
HEB. 10:5-10
LUKE 1:39-45

"When Elizabeth heard Mary's greeting, the infant leaped in her womb."

During this time of the year it is an annual family tradition of ours to revisit that classic play by Charles Dickens, *A Christmas Carol*, at our local theatre. In this adaptation we find an opening scene where Scrooge's nephew, Fred, along with his new bride Lilly, is visiting Uncle Scrooge at his offices and they are there inviting him to their home to celebrate Christmas. Lilly pleads with him to join them and tells him that his presence was missed at their recent wedding. And Scrooge replies, "Bah, humbug! You don't mean my presence—you mean my presents were missed!

And so as we gather on this fourth and last Sunday of Advent, many of us may be a bit preoccupied and possibly stressed with the buying of the presents…writing out the Christmas cards…hanging the lights…decorating the trees…going to parties and attending to all the family traditions. And all that and more—while quite exhausting—is part of the season and fine for most. I guess one could say that it is human nature for us to be focused on the presents—the gifts of Christmas. But as we gather here this morning, days before we celebrate the birth of Christ, the Church in her infinite wisdom gives us this gospel to ponder and to pray over, a gospel that perhaps will grab our attention away from the shopping and remind us that it is indeed our presence that is much more important than the presents that we give or receive.

We find Mary not focusing inward on her own pregnancy, but rather reaching out to others by setting out to see her cousin. For Elizabeth, advanced in age, home with a husband who is deaf and dumb, was now six months pregnant and would no longer be able to go and draw water from the village well, go to market to do her shopping, or to look after the crops in her garden. Keep in mind: this was not a walk around the block for Mary—rather, this was a 78-mile trek by foot and donkey by a pregnant 14 year old. And when she arrives for a three-month stay, there is no mention of any housewarming gifts in tow, no talk of food platters or wrapped baby gifts. Rather, Mary, filled with divine presence, gives Elizabeth the gift of her presence—and, as we heard today, upon her greeting the infant leapt within Elizabeth's womb.

And Elizabeth, seeing Mary is with child, calls her "the Mother of my Lord." It is interesting to note the importance given to this meeting, as it is the only time in the New Testament that there is a dialogue recorded between two women.

In a few days we will celebrate the birth of Mary's child: Jesus, the Son of God, the son of Mary, born fully human and fully divine. Our Christmas present is the perfect presence of the Christ Child. Our Christmas present is the fact that we all have the indwelling of God, which is Emmanuel—God with us. We all carry the presence of Christ.

Franciscan Richard Rohr, in his latest book, *The Naked Now*, says, "[We] still think of ourselves as mere humans trying to desperately to become 'spiritual,' when the Christian revelation was precisely that we are already spiritual and our difficult but necessary task is to learn how to become human."

In short, Rohr reminds us that we are all spiritual—we all have this indwelling—and Christ became incarnate, became fully human, in order to show us how to be human to ourselves and to others. And how did he do this? It was by being present to others. Flip through your mind for your favorite gospel story—Jesus at the well with the woman, Jesus healing the blind, Jesus dining with the sinners, Jesus calling to Peter on the water, and so on. Wherever he went, he brought the gift of his presence. And our needs are no different 2,000 years later. Everyone needs and receives that internal peace and joy that comes from the presence of God.

This is what Mary's visit did for Elizabeth. Mary's visit was gift and grace to Elizabeth. So, too, the family and friends we visit this Christmas give us an opportunity to bring the same gift and grace into their lives, to bring them closer to God, and to share with them the Spirit of God in us—the Spirit of consolation, of courage, of peace and joy, just as Mary did. It is easy to go online and order a present, or to drop in at a mall and pick up a gift—but to give the gift of ourselves, to make time to be with another, that is the gift that many people long for but do not receive at Christmas. Indeed, I do not think that there is a greater gift that we can give than that of ourselves, our presence, our time.

And how do we find the courage and the strength to do this?

The answer lies in the reason why we are gathered here: we come to this table with all of our joys and all of our sorrows to be nourished by the greatest gift Jesus gave us—his physical presence, his body and blood. Presence was so important to Jesus that at the Last Supper he instituted the Eucharist and told us to do this time and time again so that we can be fed—so that his presence can give us the strength to be present to others. Do this and remember me…remember how I was human…remember how I was present to others…remember how I forgave others…remember what I did for the least of my brothers and sisters…come, follow me.

Beginning tomorrow with the Winter Equinox, the light will increase as our days become longer and our nights will become shorter and very soon we will celebrate the birth of our Savior and Redeemer, The Lord of Lords,

The King of Kings, The Holy Lamb, The Perfect Presence. May you be that presence, that ever brightening force bringing light to those in darkness. With just a few days left in Advent, try to find time to slow down a bit…let that frazzled person in line behind you cut up to the front…don't fret if the Christmas cards don't all get out in time…and it will be okay if some presents do not arrive till after December 25th. Rather, make time for one another…make time for yourself. And never forget that the greatest present you have and the one that you can give time and time again is the presence of the God who dwells within you, the God who loves you, the God who is Emmanuel.

CHRISTMAS SEASON

NATIVITY OF THE LORD: MIDNIGHT

MICHAEL DOYLE

Isa. 9:1-6
Tit. 2:11-14
Luke 2:1-14

"Do not be afraid."

The oldest room in the world was built 5200 years ago in Ireland. It is still standing inside the center of an acre-sized hill that was built by human hands and is situated in a place called Newgrange. There is a narrow entrance into which people walk in single file through a rock-lined tunnel for sixty slightly ascending feet to the room where three shallow stone basins rest on the floor. They were probably used for the ashes of the dead. Above the entrance to all this, there is a small opening called a "roof box" that is a few square feet in size, somewhat like a lintel window above a door. At the time of winter solstice, December 21 or 22, the first ray of the sun coming over the nearest rim of the hill sends a laser-like shaft of light through that roof box and miraculously lights up the sixty-foot passageway and beams on the basins in the room.

Newgrange is much more than a tomb—it is a temple of wondrous inspiration. Our winter solstice is the day of least light and yet enough to penetrate the tunnel of darkness and light up the ashes of the dead. It is extraordinary that people 3000 years before Jesus was born could align the first ray of the rising sun with a small hole in a hill and bathe the dead remains of human life in light. Big stones had to be moved miles and big obstacles had to be overcome to prepare the way for such a wonder on this planet. So it is altogether fitting that the birth of the "Sun of Righteousness" would be aligned with the birth of the sun in the solstice of our winter.

We celebrate Christmas on December 25, in the season of least light, and John the Baptist on June 24, in the season of most light. John said, "He must increase; I must decrease." (John 3:30) We celebrate the two holy Cousins in the two great solstices of the year. So rich it all is that we must rejoice in cosmic acknowledgement.

The preparation for the birth of Jesus began with creation and continued in one way or another over all time. About 2500 years after the solar peoples of Ireland lit up their sacred space with the rising sun and some dim hope that death was not the end of us, Isaiah, the prophet, peering down the centuries was proclaiming that, "The people who have walked in darkness have seen a great light; upon those who dwelt in the land of gloom, a light has shone." (Isa. 9:1)

My childhood years were burdened by poverty of material things and light in the long winter nights was confined to one small lamp in the kitchen. Paraffin oil was rationed due to the Second World War. We couldn't afford candles, but we had them on Christmas night. There was a light in every window. It was a fearless night because there was light in the dark of every room.

Fear of the dark is more than night; the darkness of the unknown is all so frightening when humans ache for the light of understanding. Four special words form the happy messages of angels coming to this earth as God's advance team for the birth of Jesus. At least three times we hear them and they are: "Do not be afraid." First in Matthew 1:20: "Joseph, son of David, do not be afraid to take Mary." He did. In Luke 1:29, when Mary "was greatly troubled" at Gabriel's salutation, she heard: "Do not be afraid, Mary, you have found favor with God." And Mary, a human being, accepted the most awesome assignment in all creation with: "May it be done unto me," and she became the Mother of God and later gave birth to Jesus in Bethlehem, where the shepherds in the fields, humble as crossing guards in a slum, had a visit from an angel and "the glory of God shone around them." Then, their night was bright but they were in the dark as to what was happening. The angel said to them: "Do not be afraid." (Luke 2:10) They pulled themselves together and heard "good news of great joy that will be for all the people." And so, with light leaping in their eyes, "they went in haste and found Mary and Joseph and the infant lying in the manger." (Luke 2:16) And sure enough, "they made known the message," the best bit of breaking news, really good news, ever to come down the pike of the planet, or even the whirl of the universe. After the angels, "the shepherds said to one another, let us go then to Bethlehem and see." (Luke 2:15)

To celebrate Christmas, we need to go in mind to Bethlehem and see for ourselves. But, it's not with 20/20 vision that we will see, but with supreme levels of wonder. We must go, humble as shepherds in smelly clothes, who have no words. They are in silent, awestruck astonishment before the scene they saw. It was as the angel told them: "An infant wrapped in swaddling clothes and lying in the manger, a Savior has been born for you, who is Messiah and Lord." (Luke 2:1) Divinity is swaddled with humanity in an animals' food trough.

In recent times, great minds like Brian Swimme have been trying to lay a tape on the universe and have found that it is expanding faster than one could say "stardust." However, their findings are creating deep wells of wonder for humanity. That wonder helps us to bow before the mystery of God in flesh tucked into the manger of a marvelous moment in mind and soul.

St. Paul says that Jesus Christ "is the image of the invisible God, the first-born of all creation. For in Him, all things were created...in Him all things hold" (Col. 1:15,17). The matter that is the fruit of the fields of Nazareth made its way into Mary's bowl and bloodstream to form the flesh of God's incarnation. "In Him all things hold…" They do, indeed, the whole universe holds in its stretching development. "I am the light," says Jesus, whose first home on the planet was the dark walls of a womb. It will help us as we gaze in awesome astonishment at the baby in the tiny boundaries of about eight pounds, to acknowledge that our expanding universe is 78 billion light-years in diameter.

The ray of dawn that first hit the hole in the hill of Newgrange, County Meath, and lit up the ashes of the dead, had traveled several billion light years to do so. Three thousand years later, "the star that they (the magi) had seen at its rising preceded them, until it came and stopped over the place where the child was. They were overjoyed at seeing the star." (Matt. 2:9) It was the greatest "global positioning" of all time. The starlight had traveled several billion light years to reach "the place where the child was"…to reach the source of all light and life forever.

All those who heard the message of the shepherds "were amazed." (Luke 2:18) As we must be. It is all amazing. Wonder is the only way to celebrate the essence of Christmas.

HOLY FAMILY OF JESUS, MARY AND JOSEPH

REV. CAROL HOWARD MERRITT

1 SAM.1:20-22, 24-28
COL. 3:12-21
LUKE 2:41-52

"His mother treasured all these things in her heart"

It happens occasionally. My child says she will be somewhere at a certain time, and when I look for her, she is not at the specified location. I never handle these situations well. My heart beats faster, I sweat, and my head fills with every missing child report that I have heard.

I imagine a twisted kidnapper holding my child captive in a dank basement. *What if he is making her sleep on the concrete? What if he is starving her and not letting her see the sunlight? What if she is not allowed to use the bathroom and has to go in a bucket?* The worst-case scenarios crowd my thoughts as my imagination heightens my anxiety to alarming levels.

Just as the panic of what could be starts to completely take my logical brain captive, I see the back of her head. She turns around, I catch a glimpse of her smiling face and I breathe deeply. I act really cool while she tells me what happened. And then all of my fear gets boiled down to some misunderstanding about the location or time.

Perhaps not every parent immediately jumps to the most horrendous conclusions as quickly as I do, but it seems to be a common fear. Why else would a missing child story suddenly capture the country's attention and demand headline news captions for days? We find some resonance in the terror that someone we love is vulnerable and could be hurt.

Perhaps the panic is as old as Jesus. After all, we read about it in Luke. And I imagine that Mary's anxiety was heightened, even without the help of a 24-hour news cycle. Jesus had always been in danger. Mary could have been stoned while he still kicked inside of her. Then they find out that those wise men who came for a visit were unknowingly part of devious plot to kill her child. Herod sent the men to Bethlehem to gain insight on the possible competitor for his throne.

Since the Annunciation, Mary understood the importance of her child, but her adoration must have been matched by a sense of fearful foreshadowing. If she worried, it was not in vain. We are reminded of Mary's terrible love when we see the anguished beauty of Mary in the *Pieta*, holding her fully-grown son as he is taken off of the cross. She enfolds him, and as our eyes trace the lines of her mournful face, we feel the depth of sorrow of a mother who loses her child in the height of his life. The iconic image reminds us of the combination of anguish, concern, and love that binds our families.

One of the most beautiful glimpses into Mary's parenting can be found here in Luke, where we read, "his mother treasured all these things in her heart." Yes, Mary is blessed among all women, but that blessedness comes with a great burden of responsibility. And with all of that, Mary models to us a bit about parenting all children here. She shows us a bit about life in general, because Mary learned to treasure things. Even in those times when she was frustrated and angry with Jesus for disappearing and allowing her to think that the worst had happened to him, she treasured things. In the cries of sleepless nights, in the drain of exhausted days, in the thrill of first words, in the exasperation of the potty training, and in the fear of parental love, Mary treasured things.

How do we treasure things? It seems so easy to do in our current culture. We can take photos just about anywhere if we buy the right kind of phone. Or we can have special pictures taken. When I had a child, I was told to have professional photographs taken at least every three months of my child's first two years. Then we could have those images made into calendars or mugs.

We can make really special memories when we spend more money on vacations. A trip to Disneyworld will certainly be treasured. If we dress our children up in cute outfits at the theme park, then our memories will be even better.

And we can't forget to scrapbook each moment of our child's life. Even if we have to dip into our child's college fund in order to afford the hobby, it will be worth it. Because we will need acid-free paper, special scissors, and particular albums to make sure that we treasure our moments properly.

But as we buy the products that manufacture memories for our consumption, are we able to take delight in our children? It's so easy to become distracted by the commodities that seduce us with their sentimentality, but somehow Mary was able to treasure all of those things without a smartphone.

With a media that manufactures fear, we can become overwhelmed by worry and concern. With the marketing of memories, we become more interested in what we do not have than what we have. And with the simple realities of parenting, we can become so preoccupied with the sleeplessness, messiness, and chaos that we forget to treasure things. But can we learn from Mary?

Can we delight in the smell of a baby's head? Can we marvel at the tiny fingernails? Can we sit in wonder at the wisdom that each child collects through the years? Can we remember to be amazed as we watch the children around us begin to discern truth from falsehoods, understand the nuances of communication? Can we laugh as they begin to appreciate humor? Can we notice the divine favor that grows with the passing of years? Can we delight in the grace that God gives each child?

Mary treasured all of these things in her heart. Even with the anxiety of parenthood, she knew how to be amazed. May God grant us wisdom and love so that we might learn to do the same.

MARY, MOTHER OF GOD

FRAN ROSSI SZPYLCZYN

Num. 6:22-27

Gal. 4:4-7

Luke 2:16-21

"God sent his son, born of a woman."

Many years ago, I ended up befriending a woman with whom I had nothing in common. In fact, we were far apart in many ways! She was one of the "cool people" that a self-professed nerd like me might never get to know. However, academic circumstances brought us together, and we became good friends. What struck me the most about her when we first became more closely acquainted was how "human" she turned out to be. From my original point of view, this woman seemed to have it all; she appeared completely self-confident and self-possessed, she was remarkably beautiful, and she maintained an aura of perfection that seemed unattainable to us mere mortals.

Over time we got to know one another and a real friendship began to develop. This woman began to reveal just how challenging things were for her. First of all, she was not perfect, although I found that hard to believe. At that age, I believed that we were all socially divided into some "have/have not" scheme when it came to perfection. To that end, I was solidly "have not" material, but she appeared to be at the top of the perfection pyramid! Having this image thrust upon her brought forth tremendous expectations from others, expectations that she could never feel good about meeting. Whether it was from her parents, from our teachers, or from our peers, she struggled to keep the surface shiny and to keep everything moving. Inside, she was the same insecure mess that I was. What a revelation!

Our friendship was an oddity, but it did carry on for some time. Although we eventually grew apart, her friendship remains in my heart as a reminder that things are not always what they seem.

Today we celebrate the Solemnity of Mary, the Mother of God. Talk about images of perfection; no woman has more of them floating around than our Blessed Mother! Blond haired and blue-eyed, always clad in a startling shade of blue that does not seem to exist widely in nature, Mary is perfect. That part is true—she is. However, when we put so many images on her, how do we really come to know and celebrate Mary in ways that clearly show her place in our lives? Somehow I believe that if we start and stop with "perfect," we lose the deeper meaning. Remember, things are not always what they seem.

Mary has such a remarkable place in salvation history. First of all, she is the very first believer! From the moment of the Annunciation and her eternal "yes," she changes the course of history with her consent. This is a kind of perfection that we rarely consider when we think about perfection: the perfection of saying yes, with a complete commitment from a deep well of spirit.

Today we heard the Aaronic blessing in the Book of Numbers proclaiming God's loving care for God's people. The Lord is looking upon us all, looking upon us kindly and wanting to give us peace and bountiful blessings. The arc of that peace takes us from the beginning of time to the time of Mary's agreement. It was she who agreed to deliver us that peace in the life of the child that she was about to bear. Talk about things not always being what they seem!

In Mary's day, no one would have thought she was perfect. In fact, quite the opposite—she was in a compromised condition, both socially and religiously, as far from perfect as could be. Mary knew the risks, yet she still said yes, and the Lord blessed us richly as a result. This reminder that things are not always what they seem is also a message of great hope.

Continuing with that message of hope, St. Paul, in the letter to the Galatians, reminds us that "God sent the Spirit of His Son into our hearts." Not only has God done this great thing for us, but God has chosen to do so in a very particular way, "God sent His son, born of a woman." Mary was no accidental surrogate mother, but a clear choice. That choice of Mary was also her chance to make a choice, and she chose yes. Now God has come to us in human form, in the most astounding expression of love that we will ever know. No longer are we slaves, we are told, but we are children, heirs of God, through Christ.

Today Mary may seem to us the very image of perfection. We should understand that kind of perfection in a way that pushes us past superficial imagery and into the depth of understanding of what her role in our lives is meant to be. Unlike any cool image of perfection, Mary reflects the true perfection of God's love in the world. Perfection is not always what it seems, is it?

What we hear about in today's Gospel from Luke expresses something else about perfection, something much deeper. This is the dissonance of perfection against a backdrop of social stigma and shoddy surroundings. Mary and Joseph, with the child Jesus, are in the same spot as all the animals. This is far from the "ritual perfection" expected at that time. Things may look one way, but they are another.

This is a kind of perfection amidst the gritty reality of life, as Mary, Joseph and Jesus find themselves in the only spot that they can settle into, a spot that no one else will take. "Mary kept all these things, reflecting on them in her heart," says Luke. That is a very different kind of perfection than perfect skin, blond hair, as well as a certain shade of blue for Mary's clothing or her eyes. Mary was not at all like my seemingly perfect friend from 20 years ago. My friend "seemed" perfect. Our mother Mary, Mary the Mother of God is perfect.

What we find in Mary and the message that she brings us is this: God longs for us. Over time, God was interacting with God's people on a journey towards peace, reconciliation, and salvation. From the Aaronic blessing, to countless other stories in Scripture, we find God drawing closer and closer. Then God surprises us by going a whole other direction, the direction of His Son and our savior, Jesus who is Christ! With this direction, which is brought to us through Mary, the Mother of God, we are offered the greatest gift of all.

This perfect life is the perfection of God born to a woman, bringing us God's kindness and God's peace, bringing us salvation and new life, bringing us into God's family as never before. We were always God's children, but it was through Mary, who bore Jesus, that this perfection comes to us in such a profound way. And in this way we remember that things are not always what they seem.

THE EPIPHANY OF THE LORD

FR. RICHARD ROHR, O.F.M.

IsA. 60:1-6

EPH. 3:2-3A, 5-6

MATT. 2:1-12

"We saw his star at its rising and come to do him homage."

This account of the wise men only appears in Matthew's gospel. There's no other mention of three people from a foreign country to the east visiting the Christ child. And in many ways maybe we can imagine why they didn't want to tell the story. Remember, the Jewish people, no different than some Catholic people, thought they were the only ones that mattered and the only people that God loved. They believed that they were the only people that had the one true religion and all other people were hopelessly lost.

And it's a nice way to begin life—a nice way to believe. Of course, it isn't true, but for some reason, most people start that way. We all have to believe that we are special, we are chosen. And that was true of the first-century Jewish people too. So to even have told this story was a bit of an affront. Here we have three people clearly shown to be non-Jews. They were foreigner pagans. But they were called wise men because they had the big picture. They could see beyond tribal thinking of groups and nations and even religions. All they wanted was truth. And when you want truth bad enough, you don't really care who is saying the truth or where the truth is to be found even if it's beyond your group, your country, or even your religion.

You may wonder why this is not a story about the good Jews pouring out of Bethlehem to visit the newborn King. Rather, it is about three outsiders. Three supposedly lost, pagan new-agers who knew nothing about God. But they are the ones who do him homage. The ones who can recognize a light in the sky where life is to be found. The ones who follow that light at great expense and cost and time to themselves. The ones who stayed on the search. What we need are not just people who belong to religions, but people who are searching for the truth, who are searching for God, and don't assume they've already found God.

Over 20 years ago, I was giving several weeks of retreats in India. While there, I became very sick from some food I had eaten. So they put a young Hindu boy in charge of me. He was asked to care for me until I was nursed back to health. The boy waited on me day and night, making sure that my every need was met and that my little bare room was kept clean. All along, always asking me what I needed. As I lay in bed I wondered how a young man could come to such love, deeply caring for someone that he never knew. So one morning I asked him, "Who is God for you?" As most people from Asia have great reverence for older people, he said very politely, "Sir, I believe that whenever one person shows respect for another person, there is God."

Being a Hindu boy, you and I would say he was a pagan, religiously lost, with no hope of going to Heaven. And yet it was very clear to me that this very young man was filled with life. He was filled with reverence and respect for everything that was around him - even me, a foreigner. And it was in his respect for me, and I hope mine in him, that we both met God.

Brothers and sisters, this feast of the Epiphany or the manifestation shows us that God is manifest, is visible, is evident to us. God is shown forth wherever people are searching for love and light and truth. And no group in the world is going to control that search. You will find sincere and loving and generous hearts in every country and every religion, and, frankly, many who put Christians to shame for their generosity of spirit, their love of God and their love of others.

So as we begin a new year, let us challenge ourselves to be wise men and wise women. Let us journey with eyes searching to see the light, to see the truth, to see the love, to see the goodness—wherever it is found, by whatever name it carries. Let this be the year we, like the wise men, are willing to go on the same kind of stretching and perilous journeys to find the God that is always present and freely given to all.

Isa. 40:1-5, 9-11
Acts 10:34-38
Luke 3:15-16, 21-22

"You are my beloved Son, with you I am well pleased."

"*Why doesn't the Bible tell* us more about Jesus growing up?" The question came to me on three different occasions near the end of Advent and right around Christmas. After worship, in the hallway, at coffee hour, the questions had some different words attached but it was all the same. "What about Jesus as a child?" Well, there's that time in Luke when his parents took him on the 8th day to be circumcised, and then in Luke when they took him to the Temple in Jerusalem and offered a sacrifice as they presented him to the Lord.

Luke says that "the child grew and became strong, filled with wisdom and the favor of God was upon him" (2:40). And Luke is the one who tells the story about when Jesus was twelve, how his parents lost him in the temple after the festival of Passover. They found him three days later sitting among the teachers. Mary and Joseph were ticked and Jesus, he frankly sounded like a twelve year old: "Did you not know I must be in my Father's house?"

And Luke does say, "Jesus increased in wisdom and in years, and in divine and human favor" (2:52). And well, um, that's about it. If you are looking for that retrospective on the child Jesus, a kind of video montage that comes at one of those award ceremonies, if you're looking for snapshots of the Messiah growing up, sort of like that commercial for a car buying service that tells of this brilliant man who can't bring himself to go through the process of getting a car—the commercial traces his amazing life, how he thanked the doctor when he was born, and dated the school sweetheart when he was only in the 6th grade, and did open-heart surgery on the stage of a theater with a ballpoint pen as a young man—if you're looking for that kind of flash, flash, flash, yeah, that's not going to happen in the canon of scripture.

But when you are looking for what is there, when you want to get the headlines of the early years, you have to turn to Luke and his gospel. The angel Gabriel with the annunciation, Elizabeth with John kicking in her womb, the muted Zechariah starting to sing, the birth of Jesus and the swaddling clothes, the shepherds, the multitude of the heavenly host, the circumcision, the presentation, Simeon, Anna, that disappearance as a twelve year old. It is all in Luke. Like Sportscenter, the Top 10 plays in the early life of Jesus, scenes from how it all got started, that's Luke. It may not be much, but it's going to be Luke.

Which makes Luke's sparse description of the baptism of Jesus all the more surprising. The baptism of Jesus, it has to be in the Top Ten list. You would think in Luke's tribute to the early years, the baptism of Jesus may get a bit more attention. Matthew has so much more to say. John provides a firsthand account from John the Baptist. Even Mark has a bit more detail than Luke. The baptism of Jesus in Luke, it's almost an afterthought: "Now when all the people were baptized, and when Jesus also had been baptized and was praying…" If not an afterthought, it's but a phrase, the actual baptism of Jesus. No Jordan river, no "behold the Lamb of God who takes away the sin of the world." No disclaimer from John, "I need to be baptized by you." Just all the people baptized, and Jesus also had been baptized and was praying.

Oh, and by the way, from Luke, the heavens opened, the Holy Spirit descended in bodily form like a dove, and voice came from heaven. "You are my Son, the Beloved, with you I am well pleased." Right after Luke quotes the voice from heaven, the text shifts, there's a transition, one of those summary statements. "Jesus was about thirty years old when he began his work." Years wrapped in one sentence, that's so Luke. If Luke were a conductor, it is as if everything slows right there at the end of the baptismal scene; almost a ritard. "When all the people were baptized, and when Jesus himself had been baptized and was praying, and heaven was opened and the Holy Spirit descended on him in bodily form like a dove....And a voice came from heaven....you are my son.....the Beloved...with you I am....well pleased." (Wait, wait, wait)..."Jesus was about thirty years old when he began his work."

The scarcity of words, the pace that one can imagine, the baptism's place in Luke's highlights, it all becomes clear that the emphasis rests on that voice from heaven. "You are my Son, the Beloved, with you I am well pleased." Jesus was baptized? Yes. The heavens opened? Yes. The Holy Spirit fell in some way, shape, or form? Yes. But that voice, that voice from heaven. The voice proclaimed, "You are my Son, the Beloved, with you I am well pleased."

The accent on Jesus' baptism in Luke falls on God's voice from heaven. Pleased. Well pleased. With you I am well pleased. Reading Luke's highlights, the phrase "well-pleased", "pleased", "God being pleased", it rings a bell. Watching, listening, reading Luke: the early chapters, "well pleased" sounds familiar when you stop and think about it. "And suddenly there was with the angel a multitude of the heavenly host, praising God and saying, 'Glory to God in the highest heaven, and on earth peace among those with whom God is pleased.'" Every Christmas we squirm a bit when the story is read, when the angels sing, isn't it really peace on earth good will to all? Isn't the King James better, "Peace on earth, good will to men?" Peace among those whom God favors. Peace among those with whom God is pleased? Sounds a bit exclusive, a bit awkward in the age of inter-faith dialogue, a bit less than the peace everywhere we would wish for at Christmas, a bit uneasy if you're not sure you fall into the group of those whom God favors, those with whom God is pleased, pleased, well-pleased, with you I am well-pleased.

The notion of that which is pleasing to God has roots in the Old Testament practice of sacrifice. Sacrifice like Mary and Joseph offering a pair of turtledoves when presenting their newborn child in the Temple, a sacrifice intended to be pleasing to God. The prophet Micah turns that world of sacrifice upside down with his definition of sacrifice, his proclamation of what the Lord doth require of us: but to do justice, and to love kindness, and to walk humbly with our God. Lives full of justice, kindness, humility; that's what pleasing to God. Christ's sacrifice, our good works, all of it pleasing to God.

I don't know. If God is dependent on our good works to be pleased, if God has to wait for humanity's righteousness to come into full bloom in order to be pleased, well, God has and will be waiting a long, long time. God's good pleasure. Fasting described by the voice of the Lord through the prophet Isaiah, the fast chosen by God that is good, acceptable, pleasing; it is to loose the bonds of injustice, to undo the thongs of the yoke, to let the oppressed go free, to share bread with the hungry, to bring the homeless poor into the house, to clothe the naked. Pleasing to God. How's that part going in the world today? God's good pleasure. God deserves better than what we have to offer.

God's good pleasure. The notion may be rooted in the ancient world of sacrifice, an aroma pleasing to God. But it must be more than that. When that voice came from heaven, when Luke stops everything so that the reader can listen, "You are my Son, the Beloved, with you I am well pleased," it is not just a death on the cross that is foreshadowed. The image is of a Father cradling a child and blessing all of life that is to come, a mother seeing love shine back as she looks into the child's eyes, a parent with child in arms for whom time stands still and whose world is rocked and everything else pales in comparison to one sacred moment. "You are my Son, the Beloved with you I am well pleased." Not just "*This* is my Beloved Son." *You* are my Beloved Son!

It's not just sacrifice. It's everything! God looking into the dripping face of Jesus and seeing the whole big picture of creation and life and heavenly hosts and the throne of heaven. God looking at Jesus and seeing it all—glory and honor and power and might. God watching as Jesus came up from his knees and seeing justice and kindness and compassion breaking forth like the dawn. God seeing in Jesus the very plan of salvation radiant in its entire splendor. God wrapping the soaking wet Jesus in the warmth of the Holy Spirit, knowing that the magnificence of God's own mercy is shining back at that moment, glistening in the water of baptism.

One of the phrases of our theological tradition as it interprets the sacraments is this: "What is true for Christ has passed into the sacraments." Baptism. Lord's Supper: a means of grace. His grace. Conveying to us the very promise of God revealed in Jesus Christ. If that is true, Christ made real and present with us every time we splash here and eat there, that the Holy Spirit meets us here just as Christ has promised, if that is true, then every time we gather here at the fount, something of that first baptismal moment sparks anew. Something of God's good pleasure. More than our own sacrifice of praise, more than our affirmation of faith, more than our welcoming into the church, more than a washing for the once and future forgiveness of sins, it is about God's good pleasure. Pleased. Well-pleased. The very plan of salvation in all of its splendor.

It's the essence of the gospel, isn't it? Not us, but him. Not our good works, but his. Not our love, but his. Pleased. Well pleased, God pleased not just with him, but with us because of him. His birth. His life. His witness. His ministry. His justice. His righteousness. His death. His resurrection. It's everything. "You are my Son, the Beloved, with you I am well pleased." And because of you, well pleased with everyone who receives Christ's love. Glory to God in the highest and on earth peace among those with whom God is well-pleased. God's good pleasure. God looks at us and sees Jesus. That's everything!

I was visiting Josiah this week down at Children's Hospital in Philadelphia. Josiah is 2. He's been very sick but he's getting better, much better. I stop at the foot of his bed and his mother announced to the child, "Josiah, this is the big guy who baptized you." Josiah was unimpressed. He was watching Shrek. A little bit later, I sat with Josiah while his parents went for some lunch. We watched the end of Shrek together and he fell asleep, there on the bed surrounded by stuffed animals. He looked like ET in the closet hiding among all the toys. I looked at him sleeping there and I thought of all the babies I have baptized, all the people. I don't know how many. The first baby I baptized is 25 now. I looked at Josiah's face and I saw all these other faces from around the fount. God looks at Josiah's face, and God sees the face of Jesus.

LENT

ASH WEDNESDAY

DEACON GREG KANDRA

JOEL 2:12-18
2 COR. 5:20-6:2
MATT. 6:1-6, 16-18

"Rend your hearts…and return to the Lord, your God."

We all remember where we were on September 11, 2001. One of my most haunting memories, though, is the morning after.

It was impossible to get out of Manhattan—or get in. Subways and trains had stopped. There were no cabs. I had to work late for CBS, and ended up walking several blocks through a deserted midtown to spend the night in a hotel on 52nd Street. I remember crossing Broadway and looking down toward Times Square and it was empty and dark. Completely deserted, except for the cops on every corner. It was nearly two in the morning before my head hit the pillow. I awoke five hours later to the sound of sirens.

I looked out the window. You probably remember—it was another stunning September day, just like the one before. I could see the street below. Fire engines and ambulances were heading downtown. I showered, threw on my clothes, and headed downstairs.

As I passed through the lobby to check out, I saw a strange figure checking in: a fireman. He was still wearing his coat and boots. But they were barely visible.

Because he was covered, head to foot, in ash. He looked like a ghost. As he signed in, some of the ash flaked to the floor.

I've never been able to think of ashes, or Ash Wednesday, the same way. It was the most powerful and poignant reminder of what ashes really mean to us—and why this day means so much to us.

Ash Wednesday is, ultimately, all about loss. Losing part of ourselves for God. The part that's hard, or selfish, or petty. We want to burn it off, and bear the remnant, to show the world our desire to change.

The Catholic Encyclopedia tells us that Christians have been marking Ash Wednesday—and marking our foreheads—for over a thousand years now. The "day of ashes" (dies cinerum) harkens back to the eighth century.

So many things have changed in the Church over the last twelve hundred years, but this ritual has remained virtually the same. Perhaps it is one reason so many of us are here today. It's not an obligation—the Church doesn't demand it. But we can't help ourselves. It's in our theological DNA.

But perhaps there is more to it than we realize—especially now.

More than ever before, it seems, we live in an age of ashes. This soot is a reminder of the fires that have lit our world and the embers left behind from so many wars and so many ruins. Think of the fires of Hiroshima, of London, of Auschwitz, of Vietnam, of Baghdad, of New York.

We are citizens of a world on fire and this is our residue, our stain. Yet, even though we bear this mark and have left it on others, we go on. We hope. We repent. We reconcile ourselves with God. We pray. We rebuild, turning over shovels of ash, to begin again. We believe in something better to come: redemption and resurrection.

And every now and then, we witness that miracle of renewal. The cities that burned have been rebuilt. A glass tower is rising again at Ground Zero.

Soon enough, we know that after winter, there will be spring. But first there is work to do. And so, we are beginning Lent.

It starts in the middle of an ordinary week, with a thumbprint. As the day goes on, maybe we'll forget about it, and later catch a glimpse in a mirror and realize, with a shock, that we have been marked.

The question I ask you is this: what will we do about it? A lot of people we'll meet will notice the ashes and ask, "What are you giving up?"

Good question. But I like to remind myself that the first word of "giving up" is giving. It is not truly a sacrifice unless it is also, somehow, a gift. An offering of self, with no expectation of getting anything in return.

As the prophet Joel tells us today: "Rend your hearts." Open them up for the world. That is how we should spend the next 40 days. That is where penance begins.

Penance means more than just prayer and fasting, devotions and dieting. It is also a hardship. (It shares the same root as the word "penalty.") What are some of the modern hardships we find difficult to bear?

Well, try this: spend a few moments respectfully listening to someone you can't stand—or somebody that no one else likes, either. I once heard of a monk who got into some sort of trouble at a monastery. At meals, no one would sit with him—except for one other monk, who went out of his way to spend just a few minutes quietly eating with him, and letting him know that he still mattered.

That lone monk was being Christ to another. Each of us, I think, can learn from that example.

Or if that seems like too much, try this: Fold a 20-dollar bill and slip it into the poor box. Pray for a stranger or an enemy. Skip dessert and send the money to a bread line. Take time to write a letter to a soldier overseas. Visit the sick, the aging, the shut-in. Light a candle for all those who are lost, frightened, uncertain, or alone. Buy a bagel for the homeless woman you see at the train station every morning. Say a rosary for peace.

In short, begin this season of giving up…by giving.

Plant these small seeds of sacrifice. Tend them. Nurture them. And then let the roots take hold. And, in time, grace will grow.

You may well be astounded at the minor miracles that have blossomed by Easter morning.

It is all grace, amazing grace.

And it grows out of sacrifice, and prayer—and ashes.

DEUT. 26:4-10
ROM. 10:8-13
LUKE 4:1-13

"Jesus was led by the Spirit into the desert to be tempted by the devil."

I once heard a Presbyterian pastor recount a discussion held at a session meeting in Western Pennsylvania. The agenda item had to do with stewardship, mission, and the budget. Apparently some elders were concerned that the proposed budget was too generous in the percentage that was being given outside the walls of the church. Some were convinced the pastor was being too bold and a bit presumptuous in her stewardship preaching and her claim that Presbyterians still believed in tithing.

They flat out told her they were offended that she would offer an indictment of their giving, using statistics that indicated that the majority in the church gave less than ten dollars a week. Those who tried to justify their frustration with the church budget and the preaching made the attempt to turn to scripture. One elder reminded everyone that the Bible said that the love of money was the root of all evil. He said it again with emphasis to insure those around the table got the point; not money, just the love of money. Another elder proudly quoted that God helps those who help themselves. The first elder, buoyed by the encouragement of his colleague, went another step; "Yes, doesn't it say charity begins at home." And one more elder around the table tossed in another, "Yes, the Bible says to thine own self be true."

The pastor tried to stay calm, but had lost her patience. "You can try to argue about the Bible using quotes, even with chapter and verse. But if you're going to try that approach when it comes to stewardship and giving, your position will lose every time. Charity begins at home; that was Terence, a century and half before Christ. God helps those who help themselves. That was Ben Franklin. To thine own self be true, that's William Shakespeare, Hamlet, Act I, scene 3." She finished with the old affirmation that even the devil can quote scripture but then added to it. "Unlike you," she said, "the devil gets it right!"

When it comes to the temptation of Jesus I can imagine that the devil did, in fact, provide Jesus with the chapter and the verse. The gospels just don't record that part. William Sloan Coffin, the legendary preacher and spokesperson for peace at Yale University and Riverside church, expressed his frustration at those who toss scripture around like after dinner mints in the midst of the most painful of human experiences. The experience came in the aftermath of his son's death in a car accident. In a published sermon he lamented some of the clergy types who offered him quotes instead of comfort. "I felt some...were using comforting words of scripture for self-protection, to pretty up a situation whose bleakness they simply couldn't face. But like God herself, scripture is not around for anyone's protection, just for everyone's unending support!" Coffin gave thanks for those who come to the rescue and don't quote anybody. They just come to hold your hand, or bring some food, and don't say anything.

The story of Jesus being led by the Spirit into the wilderness to be tempted by the devil most often comes with a traditional interpretation. Forty days of preparation that preceded a public ministry of preaching, teaching, and healing. The devil offers personal, physical temptation: you can turn these stones into bread and satisfy your hunger. The next temptation comes with political power: I will give you authority over all these kingdoms of the world. And the last temptation has religious overtones as the battleground shifts to the roof of the temple and the devil questions the relationship with and the protection of God.

The dare of temptation: physical, political, spiritual. Each time the response comes from Jesus in the form of a reference to scripture, each time from the Old Testament book of Deuteronomy. Not bread alone. Worship the Lord your God. Don't test the Lord. Three temptations. Three citations. The conversation stops. But in those forty days in the wilderness there had to be more tests from the devil involved. The gospels only record three. The Book of Hebrews concludes that Jesus was "tempted in every way." There had to be much more to that story of Jesus and the devil. But the conversation finally stopped when the devil started quoting scripture. At least in Luke the conversation ends when the devil dares Jesus with Psalm 91:ll-12.

Have you ever thought about starting a list in your mind of the odd places, or the inappropriate places, where you have heard scripture being quoted? In a Disney movie, for instance. The movie is "The Jungle Book." The big old bear lays wounded on the ground and his friends mourn and the quote comes, "No greater love than this, to lay down one's life for a friend." That comes from Jesus in the Gospel of John. If you hear a scripture quote in a political speech you ought to run to your Bible and read it in context. And you may join me in despair the next time you hear someone trying to offer comfort to a hurting soul by grasping for those words from Romans, "All things work for good for those who love God."

The account of the temptation of Jesus is told in all three of the synoptic gospels. However, Luke provides a unique twist that is worth pondering. Mark barely takes the time to mention the encounter at all. But he does write about how the angels waited on Jesus there in the wilderness as he was tempted by the devil and lived with the wild beasts. Matthew, like Luke, unpacks the story a bit more. After the devil departed, Matthew reports that the angels came suddenly and waited on him. There are no angels in Luke. Here in the temptation story as told by Luke there are no angels. You know Luke is not averse to angels. In this gospel angels pronounce both the Lord's birth and the Lord's resurrection. But here in the wilderness, nothing. The devil offers that quote from Psalm 91. Jesus ends the conversation. "Do not put the Lord your God to the test." Of course, we think the test comes with the invitation to jump from the temple. Maybe the test Jesus objects to is the devil having a go at chapter and verse. And Luke tells us "when the devil had finished every test, he departed from him until an opportune time." No angels. No miraculous comfort from heaven. Just a foreshadowing of what is yet to come.

According to Luke, the devil departed until an opportune time. Of course you know the opportune time: that night in the garden when he was betrayed by someone he loved, when his friends fell asleep and sweat oozed from his brow in drops of blood. That opportune time when he hung from a cross, when he went willingly to his death while people stood below and dared him to save himself. Those three days in total separation from God, that's where he descended into hell. That opportune time.

With reference to the opportune time Luke lets the reader know there is more to this story yet to come. An invitation to sit back and look at the whole picture of the gospel. The devil wants to dare Jesus by quoting scripture. Luke invites the reader to encounter the truth of the suffering, the betrayal, the denial, and the death of the Son of God.

I have decided to give up something for Lent. That's not a typical spiritual discipline for me. I think I will give up those confrontations with people who want to argue by quoting chapter and verse from scripture. Like the person who wanted to argue sacramental theology with me by quoting John 6:53. Or the longtime member of my Thursday Bible study who thought he was always just one verse away from getting me to believe capital punishment was okay. Or the well-intentioned, if not incredibly insensitive pastor, who sat in on the night class at the local high school on science and theology that I volunteered to teach and proceeded to offer his own justification of creationism by citing chapter and verse over and over again while I had an out of body experience and completely left the room.

Of course, as a church full of Presbyterians, we're at a disadvantage when we're still trying to figure out what comes from the Bible and what comes from Ben Franklin. So instead of leafing for chapter and verse, why not be intentional in a community that yearns to dwell in the Book of Psalms? Instead of grabbing for the highlighter on your desk, why not seek to explore a depth to this Word that surely comes by the power of the Holy Spirit in the texts of scripture, in the event of preaching in the context of worship, and in the person and work of Jesus Christ? And instead of choosing to dare one another with chapter and verse, why not hope to have the eyes to see the gospel of Jesus Christ. Which means, of course, that we are called to ponder again the truth of the suffering, the betrayal, the denial, and the death of the Son of God.

A professor of mine in seminary once told me that if he were going back to the parish, he would look for a congregation that was looking to share in communion more often, not less. I always assumed that he was talking about the worship life of the church. The Table does sit at the center of our life together in Word and Sacrament. But here we are invited to look at the whole story and to remember anew the Lord's death and resurrection. The Table should sit at the center when we think about faith, when we struggle to grow, when we want to learn, when we want to see and experience the truth. Like Luke, I don't see many angels waiting to serve us in the wilderness. I guess that topic is for another day. But I do know of an invitation that comes from a Savior. He bids you to come and eat and drink.

GEN. 15:5-12,17-18
PHIL. 3:17-4:1
LUKE 9:28B-36

"While he was praying, his face changed in appearance and his clothing became dazzling white."

*T*homas Merton, the Trappist monk, was standing on a street corner in downtown Louisville when a transfiguration hit him. The city seemed to glow. "There is no way of telling people," he marveled, "that they are walking around shining like the sun. There are no strangers. The gate of heaven is everywhere!"

Sometimes, when we least expect it, God opens the eye of our soul and we, too, behold the divine within and around us. It wasn't Jesus who was transfigured on that mountain. Like Merton, it was the apostles who were! For just a moment they saw beyond appearances to the life and truth and beauty that are really there.

Transfiguration, like beauty, is in the eye of the beholder. The mystic Meister Eckhart put it this way: "We see God with the same eye God sees us." The apostles were blessed with a moment of seeing that comes from within. At one time or another it comes to everyone.

Transfiguration isn't a spectacular special effect. It is an integral affect, a sweet glimpse of heaven that comes when we're not looking for it. Have you ever beheld a baby at sleep or an old person at peace and realized that there is more to heaven and earth than meets the eye and for a moment understood that there are no strangers, that all of us are somehow, mysteriously, one? That is a transfiguration. Have you ever been reading a spiritual book when suddenly your eyes open wide at an insight you've never had before? The book falls from your hand; you are at peace. That is a transfiguration. Have you ever chased fly balls in spring or swam in a lake in August or walked city streets on a cool autumn day or watched snowflakes fall outside your window on Christmas day, and felt what the disciples felt? It is good for me to be here! That is transfiguration. It's better than spectacular—it is wonderful. Transfiguration is the opening of our everyday mind to the heaven that is already here.

That's what happened to the apostles. As dazzling as the telling of their story is, it is also what sometimes happens to us. We can't make transfiguration happen. Jesus said that it is God living in us who makes it happen (John 14:10). All we can do is be interested in being with Jesus, as the apostles were that day. Transfiguration is a grace that comes to us when we aren't looking for it, on the spot where we are standing, not the place where we want to be. It lasts only a moment, but changes the way we look at the world forever. Its memory is what keeps us going when the world becomes a dark place.

I love the story of the Zen fishmonger who had experienced transfiguration but still peddled fish and still smelled of fish, and whose friends asked, "What's so great about your life now?" He answered, "Well, everything is exactly the same as it was before, except that sometimes wherever I go the dead trees come to life."

When the world becomes dark, we remember: once we knew, God is everywhere. And we stumble forward in the knowledge that, despite appearances, Christ is here and Christ will come again. And we will see him in the most ordinary places.

In the movie *Field of Dreams*, the spirit of Ray Kinsella's dad asks his son, "Is this heaven?"

"No," he answers. "It's Iowa."

Iowa, like God, is everywhere. Transfiguration is awareness that "we live and move and have our being in God" (Acts 17: 18). It is knowing we are literally "in Love" (1 John 4: 7-8). It is the gift of wisdom Moses received when he, like the apostles, climbed a mountain and realized he was "standing on holy ground" (Exodus 3:5). It is what Elijah's servant beheld after the prophet prayed, "O Lord, open his eyes and let him see!" When the servant looked up he saw the hillside around Elijah on fire with light (2 Kings 6:17). Again, as spectacular as are the biblical tellings, transfigurations are normal events built into everyone's spiritual DNA. Here is the paradox of transfiguration: Moses' Mount Horeb was as familiar to him as the one the disciples stood on was to them, and Elijah's hillside was as commonplace to the servant as the plains were to Ray Kinsella when he envisioned a ball field. What burned was not a bush but the gift of vision in Moses' eye. What blazed was not a hillside but a revelation in the disciple's mind. That's how it was for the apostles in the transfiguration story, and that's how it is for us: simple, miraculous, and as natural as birth.

Thomas Merton wrote, "Life is this simple: we are living in a world that is absolutely transparent and the divine is shining through it all the time. This is not just a nice story or a fable, it is true."

What happens next is what happens to us every time we receive a transfiguration. Just as soon as the apostles see Jesus as he really is, Peter makes a Big Deal out of it. He shouts out, "Let's make three dwellings, one for you, one for Moses, and one for Elijah!" and a cloud comes over them. The vision vanishes as fast as it appeared. The apostles were asleep before they saw the Christ in Jesus and slipped back into their fog as soon as they tried to freeze what they saw. Transfigurations are like that. They fall to pieces as soon as we try to pin them against the wall of our mind like a butterfly. We don't catch the butterfly, the butterfly catches us. It alights on our shoulder without our bidding. A transfiguration comes to us on colorful see-through wings. As soon as we try to capture it or make an idol of it or take credit for it, a cloud of ego hides it.

That's the way of transfiguration. So don't worry, there's no one to blame. Blessings, like thieves, come in the middle of the night, and just as quickly get chased away. To paraphrase another Eastern sage: Before transfiguration, mountains are mountains and rivers are rivers. The moment we experience a transfiguration, mountains are no longer mountains and rivers cease to be rivers. After the transfiguration, mountains are again mountains and rivers once again rivers.

As it was for the disciples, so it is for us. We simply move on with the memory in our hearts. Until the dead trees come to life again. And then a new memory reinforces the first.

Mountains may be mountains to you right now. Someday when you least expect it, they will cease to be mountains, if only for a moment. The key to transfiguration is to not be interested in having one. To paraphrase the first law Moses brought down from a mountain: "Thou shalt have no other interest before interest in God and in Jesus Christ whom God has sent." That is the gateway to heaven.

3ᴿᴰ SUNDAY OF LENT

FR. WILLIAM BAUSCH

Exod. 3:1-8a, 13-15	
1 Cor. 10:1-6, 10-12	*"Repent and believe the good news."*
Luke 13:1-9	

A thumbnail lesson for today: Did you ever wonder how Lent began? It began in the early centuries when, as more and more people wanted to become Christians, a formal process of preparation was developed for them, a process designed to culminate in the candidates' baptism on early Easter morn. This arduous process, often lasting for years, ended with a final forty-day marathon of studying, fasting, scrutiny, prayer, and charity before baptism was finally administered on Easter. It was this final forty-day push for the candidates that became our standard Lent for all Christians. And the designated word "Lent" was a good one: It comes from an old word meaning "lengthen." It refers to the lengthening of daylight, the start of spring and therefore new beginnings, the whole idea of Lent.

In the course of history, Ash Wednesday was attached to Lent as an official introduction, a name given by Pope Urban in 1099. It could start as early as February 4 or as late as March 10, depending on the Easter date, which in turn depends on the moon's cycle.

End of thumbnail. But now we have to add that, unfortunately, during the course of the centuries, Lent's purpose and meaning hopped the track as its main focus moved to penance, to giving up something, to fasting. By defining penance and fasting as Lent's exclusive purpose we lost what it was really all about. The real purpose, the real goal of Lent goes back to

Jesus' words often translated as, "Repent and believe the good news." But the word translated as "repent" in the original Greek is *metanoia*, which really means "a change of mind and heart."

In other words, Lent's intent doesn't have anything to do with penitence and fasting as such, but with changing our way of life. Fasting, penance, and good deeds are only the means, not the end. The end, the goal of Lent is transformation: to be a different person, to lose our self-centeredness and the habit of measuring everything by our needs and feelings in order to become a caring, compassionate person.

Lent, then, is about a radical change of mind and heart, of learning to see the world as God sees it, of becoming—let me use an old word here—noble; of learning to withdraw from the relentless narcotics of consumption and greed, of me-first, and simply becoming a good human being—again, to use an old word—a saint. Once more, Lent is about transformation, when someday kindness and charity will become second nature to us.

Lent's charter story is Ebenezer Scrooge, an Easter rather than a Christmas figure. His terrible penitential visions were but the means for his transformation from a miserly skinflint to a compassionate human being. Scrooge is not the perfect Christmas character, he is the perfect lenten pilgrim.

So, at the end of Lent we are not to tally up on our spiritual scorecard how many things we gave up or how many devotions we took part in, how many good deeds we did. At the end of Lent what matters is if all these things brought a change of heart and mind, a transformation.

And that brings us to our final point. Transformation indeed is the goal of Lent, but the truth is that transformation is a slow, quiet affair that usually takes place as a result of repeated small moments, not the one-time big ones, and we've got to get over our fantasies that it will be otherwise. By that I mean that, like Christian Walter Mittys, we tend to fantasize that someday we will be part of a mighty drama and all the world will applaud and we will be different as a result. We will discover a cure for cancer. Out of nowhere we will step in front of the president or pope and take the bullet. We will pray over a person and they will be cured. We will find a way to reverse global warming. We will be nominated the American Idol of the year who on TV announces to a stunned world that we are giving up fame and fortune to become a priest or a nun to work among the poor in Africa. You name your own fantasy, but there we are, on the cover of *Time* magazine, transformed from nobody to somebody.

It's a fun but a futile fantasy. Transformation is seldom instant: very few St. Pauls are knocked down by a vision. Rather, transformation is a result of many little acts of kindness, unnoticed charities, secret prayers, quiet compassions.

Okay, it's story time, time to let a story say what I just said, only more memorably. Listen.

It's a story of a night-shift cabbie who, on a late August night, picked up a woman. He was responding to a call from a small brick complex in a quiet part of town and he assumed that, as usual, he was being sent to pick up some hung-over partiers or someone who just had a fight with a lover, or a worker heading to an early shift in the industrial part of town.

When he arrived at 2:30 AM the building was dark except for a single light in a ground floor window. Now, under the circumstances, most drivers would just honk once or twice, wait a minute, and then drive away. But this cabbie was different. He had seen too many impoverished people who depended on taxis as their only means of transportation or people who needed assistance. So he got out, walked to the door, and knocked.

"Just a minute," answered a frail, elderly voice.

He could hear something being dragged across the floor and, after a long pause, the door opened. There was small woman in her eighties wearing a blue print dress and a pillbox hat with a veil pinned on it, looking for all the world like somebody out of a 1940s movie. By her side was a small nylon suitcase.

He got a glimpse of the apartment that looked as if no one had lived in it for years; the furniture was covered with sheets. There were no clocks, knickknacks, or utensils on the counters. In the corner was a cardboard box filled with photos and glassware.

"Would you carry my bag to the car?" the woman asked. So he took the suitcase to the cab, then returned to assist the woman who took his arm as they walked slowly toward the curb. When they got into the cab, she gave him an address, then asked, "Could you drive through downtown?"

"It's not the shortest way," he answered.

"Oh, I don't mind," she said, "I'm in no hurry. I'm on my way to a hospice." When he looked in the rearview mirror he noticed her eyes were glistening. "I don't have any family left," she continued. "The doctor says I don't have very long."

The cabbie then quietly reached over and shut off the meter. "What route would you like to take?" he asked.

For the next two hours, they drove through the city. She showed him the building where she had once worked as an elevator operator. They drove through the neighborhood where she and her husband had lived when they were newlyweds. They pulled up in front of a furniture warehouse that had once been a ballroom where she had gone dancing as a girl. Sometimes she'd ask the cabbie to slow down in front of a particular building or corner and would sit staring into the darkness, saying nothing.

As the first hint of sun was lighting up the horizon, she suddenly said, "I'm tired. Let's go now."

They drove in silence to a small convalescent home. Two orderlies came out to the cab. They were solicitous and intent, watching her every move. They were obviously expecting her.

The cabbie opened the trunk and took the small suitcase to the door. The woman was already seated in a wheelchair. "How much do I owe you?" she asked, reaching into her purse.

"Nothing," he said.

"You have to make a living," she protested.

"There are other passengers," he responded.

Almost without thinking, he bent over and gave her a hug. She held him tightly. "You gave an old woman a little moment of joy," she said. "Thank you." He squeezed her hand then walked into the dim morning light. Behind him, a door shut. It was the sound of the closing of a life.

Now let the cabbie finish this story in his own wise words:

I didn't pick up any more passengers that shift. I drove aimlessly, lost in thought. For the rest of that day, I could hardly talk. What if that woman had gotten an angry driver or one who was impatient to end his shift. What if I had refused to take the run, or had honked once, then driven away? On a quick review, I don't think that I have done anything more important in my life.

Then he added a capsule of this homily. He said, "We're conditioned to think that our lives revolve around the great moments. But truly great moments often catch us unaware, beautifully wrapped in what others may consider a small one." Transformation, friends, is the goal of Lent and it's Lent's small acts of kindness that get you there.

Taken from Once Upon a Gospel: Inspiring Homilies and Insightful Reflections *by William J. Bausch (New London, CT: Twenty-Third Publications), 2008.*

4TH SUNDAY OF LENT

FR. PAUL HOLMES

JOSH. 5:9A, 10-12
2 COR. 5:17-21
LUKE 15:1-3, 11-32

"Everything I have is yours."

If only I could find the right words this day, I'd like to put an end to the worst thinking that Christians can do. We're almost famous for it—or maybe I should say "infamous." It's a real shame, too. Because it isn't Christian at all.

You and I are just like that Prodigal Son. We act like him—and worse, we think like him, too. It's his "thinking" that I'm focusing on this morning. The kind of thinking that says, "I've done something really bad. And it wouldn't surprise me a bit if my Father stopped loving me for it." Many of us have the same fear that the Prodigal Son has—that somehow our misbehavior disqualifies us from being loved.

Well, that's got to stop today. Right now. Today is Laetare Sunday— "Be Joyful" Sunday. We're halfway through Lent, and we should be joyful that we're that much closer to Easter!

So, how can I say it? What's it going to take? How can I get us to stop the kind of bad thinking that the Prodigal Son does as he traces his steps back home? (I'd like to find a way to stop our bad *deeds*, too, but it's our bad thoughts that make us most like the Prodigal Son.) It's "thinking" that we can do something to lose God's love. It's "thinking" that God will stop loving us—ever! Or stand with his arms crossed, making us crawl back to him on our hands and knees. Or, worse, that we've lost the privilege of being called his daughters and sons.

Next to the story of the Good Samaritan, the story of the Prodigal Son is Jesus' most famous parable. It's rich and vivid, and it's got a lot to tell us about what the relationship between God and us is really like. And it's shocking, too (when you come to think of it). When we eavesdrop on the son as he's talking to himself on the way home—when Jesus tells us this young man plans on asking to be treated like a *servant* instead of a *son*—Jesus is setting us up! He's preparing us for that big moment, when the father—when God—*doesn't* act the way we think he's going to act. It's as if the father doesn't even hear what his son has to say! Because he's already kissing him and hugging him! He's not listening to all that drivel his son memorized on the way home.

It's party time! And nothing the son says is going to keep his father from celebrating. Nothing. *This story*, more than any other, tells us that there's *nothing* we can do that would get God to stop loving us!

Notice what the father *didn't* do in this story: When his son asks for his inheritance—the father *doesn't* kick him out for being so ungrateful. When his son takes his inheritance, the father doesn't hire a private investigator to take compromising photographs. And when his son finally comes back, the father *doesn't* make him crawl on his knees and beg for mercy and he *doesn't* tell him to join the servants. And when his older son gives him a very good argument to reconsider this Welcome Home Party, the father *doesn't* change his mind!

No, no. That's the way we would act if we were in the same situation! When we look at what the Father *doesn't do*, we can come to only *one* conclusion: There's *nothing* we can do that will get God to stop loving us; or to stop waiting for us to come to our senses and return to him; or to throw the biggest party this side of heaven when we finally come back!

So...What's it going to take? What words can I offer to get us to stop thinking the way the Prodigal Son thinks?

How about: Come to Reconciliation this week! *Be joyful* today that God is waiting for us to come back to him. No matter what we say—no matter what sins we've committed—he's *not* going to disown us. There's a big party in our future! And nobody's going to talk him out of it.

Like the Prodigal Son, all we have to do is show up!

Isa. 43:16-21
Phil. 3:8-14
John 8:1-11

"Go, and from now on do not sin any more."

S *tones! I'd like us to* think about stones this morning! If you were to read ahead in this chapter of John's Gospel, just after Jesus convinces this crowd to drop their stones and walk away from the woman caught in adultery, you'd read about a different crowd picking up stones again—this time, to throw at Jesus himself! This chapter in John might just as well be called the Chapter of Stones!

All these stone-throwers in the Gospel of John are anonymous. But in the Acts of the Apostles, you'll remember that a few years after the Resurrection, a crowd gathers around the deacon Stephen—and, here, St. Luke tells us, the crowd is successful; they stone Stephen to death. And he also tells us that the stone-throwers laid their cloaks at the feet of the future St. Paul. How quickly a crowd can become judge, jury, and executioners. How easy to become swept up in righteous anger. How terrible the consequences when people take stones—and the law—into their own hands.

Even though St. John's "Chapter of Stones" might have us thinking about the "terror" of stones, I would like all of us this morning to think of a different kind of stone altogether. In the ancient world, a large stone was always needed to seal up a tomb. And you and I know that when Jesus was carried down off the cross, a man named Joseph of Arimathea helped lay our dead Savior into a tomb "hewn from rock" and then rolled a huge stone at the entrance to seal it. And do you know what else was sealed up in that tomb?

All of our sins. The sins of the Prodigal Son. The sins of the Woman Caught in Adultery. Your sins. And my sins.

When Mary Magdalene was returning to that tomb early Sunday morning, she was worried about who was going to roll that huge stone away for her. You see: stones, both large and small, can be a real problem. Mary couldn't have imagined what had happened. Her dead Savior, now alive— and all our sins, now forgiven—had already burst forth from that tomb. The large stone that was supposed to have sealed our Savior and our sins in that tomb forever—that stone was no obstacle for God.

As much as we might want to keep our sins all locked up, all sealed up in the tomb of our hearts, the Resurrection demands that the huge stone we've used to seal up our sins must be rolled away. All so that Salvation and Forgiveness and New Life can burst forth. Let's think about that huge stone at the entrance of our hearts. Let's ask God to roll it away with the power of God's forgiveness and mercy. Like Mary Magdalene on the way to the tomb on Easter morning, we might be thinking that we're somehow responsible for rolling that huge stone away ourselves. But let's remember that that's just plain impossible. It was impossible for her. And it's impossible for us.

Only God can roll the stone at the entrance of our hearts away.

So, I beg you: Go to confession! Sometime before Easter, let's allow the power of the Resurrection to roll away that heavy stone. We mustn't try to take the law, or that stone, into our own hands. We have a merciful Savior—no jury, no executioner. Let's give him a chance to be a merciful judge. Let's let him ask, "Is there no one left to condemn you? Then neither do I condemn you!"

We've got two weeks before Christ bursts from the tomb on Easter. Let's make a promise right now to get to confession! There's no better way to welcome the Resurrection on Easter Sunday than to write a happy ending to the Chapter of Stones in our own lives. Let's give the Lord a chance to roll away that stone at the entrance of our hearts.

PALM SUNDAY

DEACON GREG KANDRA

LUKE 19:28-40
ISA. 50:4-7
PHIL. 2:6-11
LUKE 22:14-23:56

"He opens my ear that I may hear"

We have just heard the climax of the Greatest Story Ever Told. We hear it every Palm Sunday, and we will hear it again on Good Friday. It is a story of monumental suffering and love that has been proclaimed from pulpits around the world for centuries.

It speaks for itself. There's nothing I can add to what we've all just heard. But I would like to share just one thought about something that is a vital and meaningful part of this weekend. It is the part, in fact, that gives this Sunday its name.

Last week, I stopped into a little fast food place on Prospect Park West in Brooklyn, near my office, called "Hot Diggity Dog." It probably won't surprise you to learn it's not a vegetarian place. Anyway, behind the counter, there was a rosary hanging on the wall, along with some postcards and pictures from around the world. And tucked in among them was a small folded cross, a cross made of palm leaves—a remnant from Palm Sunday past.

You find these in the unlikeliest of places. But that was a sign, I think, of the deep attachment we have to our palms. People fold these and save them, decorate their homes with them. When we were growing up, I usually threw mine out. But my sister used to keep hers behind her bedroom mirror. You sometimes see cab drivers who have them tucked in the visors of their cars, along with maps and unpaid parking tickets.

But we shouldn't think of these palms as just one more "Catholic thing" hanging on a wall or tucked behind a holy picture.

These palms tell another part of the story that we just read.

It is our story, yours and mine.

Five weeks ago, we stood in this church and received ashes. We were reminded of our mortality, our sinfulness, our need for penance and prayer. But those ashes weren't just scraped together from the bottom of somebody's fireplace. They were the remnants of burned palms.

Today we stand here again, five weeks older. Maybe, hopefully, five weeks wiser. And we hold in our hands new palms. New growth. And it begs the question: How have we grown since that one Wednesday in February?

What have we learned?

How have we changed?

And what will we do with the promise, the potential that we now hold in our hands?

Our hope and our prayer is that we have been renewed during these weeks. And, just maybe, these leaves can serve to remind us of that.

Lent is bracketed, bookended, by palms, the loss and destruction of them at the beginning, and the green new leaves—restoration—at the end. Ultimately, that is what these weeks are about. Burning away, clearing out, and cultivating something new. That is Lent.

So, take these palms. Let them be a reminder of this week that we are beginning, the holiest week of the year.

But we shouldn't just leave it at that. Don't just tuck them behind a holy picture and take them for granted. Let them also serve as a challenge. And a remembrance.

They challenge us to remember Christ's suffering and death—the triumph of that ride into Jerusalem and the tragedy of Calvary.

They challenge us to remember our role in that passion—that what Christ suffered, he suffered for us.

But they also challenge us to remember what will become of these palms…and become of us.

As we heard five weeks ago: Remember that you are dust and to dust you will return. The ashes were washed away. But these palms stay with us, offering silent testimony, bearing witness, calling on us not to forget what we are and what we will be.

That is what our Lenten pilgrimage has been about.

My prayer this Palm Sunday is that we carry that idea with us, just as we carry these palms.

Because in a sense, each of us this day holds our future in our hands.

What will we do with it?

HOLY THURSDAY

RICHARD G. MALLOY, S.J.

EXOD. 12:1-8, 11-14 | *"That as I have done for you,*
1 COR. 11:23-26 |
JOHN 13:1-15 | *you should also do."*

S hrek and Jennifer Lopez were sitting in a bar chatting. Shrek was
wondering if he was the strongest ogre in the world. J.Lo was wondering if she was the most attractive woman on earth. In walk George
Clooney and Brad Pitt. They want to know who is the best looking man
alive. So Shrek suggests they all go and consult the "magic mirror on the
wall." They agree to meet at the bar the next night to report their findings.
The next night Shrek comes in, and he's all smiling because the magic
mirror told him he is the strongest ogre on earth. And J.Lo comes in all
happy because the magic mirror told her she's the best looking gal in the
world. George Clooney and Brad Pitt show up and they are all mad. They
want to know, "Who the heck is Fr. Rick Malloy?"

I'm always a little chagrined that that joke gets such a big laugh!

How are we transformed into people who are not just strong and good
looking, but into people who can live with God forever? Not by being the
most famous, or the best at what we do, or by being higher up the ladder
than someone else. We are transformed by our service to others.

We cooperate with God's salvific activity by washing one another's feet.
Jesus challenges us on this the eve of his passion and death: "Do you
understand what I just did for you?" He doesn't ask, "Do you understand
what I am going to do for you on Friday?" He wants to know if we un-

derstand the significance of his prophetic action at the Passover meal. He wants us to realize the meaning of the washing of the feet. As Jesus served, so must we.

In John's gospel there is no Last Supper, just the multiplication of the loaves. As in that miracle, at the Last Supper Jesus chooses to serve rather than be served. Priesthood is all about service. When I was ordained a "transitional" deacon, the bishop reminded us that we would always be deacons. As priests, we are not to forget the diaconal call to serve.

A campus minister with whom I serve at the University of Scranton sent these words to me when I asked, "What should I tell people on Holy Thursday?" For her, service is all about bending.

> "Holy Thursday—the image of washing someone's feet. We romanticize it sometimes, it's all nice and holy to serve. We don't often talk about the fact that being of service requires one to bend— again, think of the image of washing feet; Jesus has to bend over to do so. As a mom I bend over a lot—to pick up heavy children (which often makes my back and bending over painful after lifting 25–35 lb. children over and over again)—I bend down to pick up toys off the floor, clean up messes, pick up laundry, remove the new puppy's teeth from some household object she is chewing, etc. It is not romantic and I am certainly not thinking I am "washing feet" in those moments. So on Holy Thursday, I would like to be affirmed in all the bending we do as parents, employees, friends, in order to be of service. The list could go on and on in terms of examples of the "bending" we do for other people—staying late at work when a family is in crisis or a student needs help, taking time to plan an event for our children's school, listening to an extended family member who is struggling as we share over a cup of coffee, etc. Compared to the ritual we envision on Holy Thursday, we

don't often connect those moments with holiness or service in the name of Christ, but they are. And even more comforting is the fact that Holy Thursday reminds us that Jesus—our God—knows what it is like to bend over; he knows what it is like to strain your back to serve, to love someone else freely. Jesus knows it is hard work and that we need encouragement—so enter the Eucharist. We are not alone and we are given the gift of Eucharist to keep us going, to nourish us, to bring us a sense of peace and again to remind us we are not alone when we want to throw our hands up in the air and say, 'My back hurts, I'm tired of all the "bending."' Could go on and on—again just thoughts from my shower, as that's one of the few quiet "prayer" moments I will get today."

Another member of our campus ministry team focused in on the table lesson of Holy Thursday.

"If you ask me, Holy Thursday is about the communal act of breaking bread...as Paulette always says at a celebration, 'Like Jesus called us to do, we come together to break bread.' I'm one who often reflects on the Last Supper and who was sitting around the table. Who do we invite to sit at our table? Would Jesus sit with immigrants? Would Jesus sit with people of different races, political preferences, sexual orientations? Do we truly embrace Christ's call to communal bread breaking? Are we disciples if we do not embrace our community? How can we fulfill God's call as humbly and selflessly as Christ did, without any agenda?

Makes a lot of sense to me. Holy Thursday is about Eucharist, giving thanks together, calling one another to self-sacrificing service, and then coming together to the table of the Lord to receive food for the journey. We both wash one another's feet and feast together.

The fact that Jesus washes the disciples' feet is shocking. Peter's reaction expresses the incongruity of the moment. What would be an image of washing feet today?

Years ago, I was looking for a summer job after my sophomore year of college. My sister, a nursing student, had gotten a job as a nurse's aide at a nursing home in our neighborhood. I went over there looking for work as a dishwasher, a job I'd done at a restaurant during high school. The gal hiring workers told me they didn't need dishwashers, but they needed orderlies. I asked how much it paid, and it was the same hourly wage. So I said, "Sure."

When I got home my sister almost busted a gut laughing. "Do you know what orderlies do?" I really didn't have a clue. But I soon learned. Orderlies wash feet and every other area of the body. Orderlies give enemas, clean up after people, change diapers—big diapers on old folks' bodies. The closest thing to washing feet that we have in our society is the service of nurses' aides and orderlies who take care of our elderly family members in nursing homes.

Service in that nursing home awakened in me a vocation to the priesthood. Jesus calls us to wash one another's feet. The gift of his body and blood is food that nourishes our loving works of service to one another. Come and receive, and let us pray.

GOOD FRIDAY

DEACON GREG KANDRA

Isa. 52:13-53:12
Heb. 4:14-16; 5:7-9
John 18:1-19:42

"He shall see the light in fullness of days"

*S*ixty years ago, the psychiatrist Viktor Frankl wrote a best-selling book about his experiences as a prisoner in Auschwitz. *Man's Search for Meaning* is considered to be a classic about the worst nightmare of the last century. Frankl describes how men, women and children coped with the horrors of the camp—how they were able simply to survive, day after day, week after week.

At one point he tells the haunting story of a woman who knew she was going to die in just a few days. Despite that, he says, she was remarkably calm, even cheerful. One morning, Frankl approached this woman and asked her how she did it. How was she able to keep her spirits up? The woman told him that she had come to a deeper appreciation of spiritual things during her time in the camp.

Then, he writes: "Pointing through the window of the hut, she said, "This tree here is the only friend I have in my loneliness." Through the window, she could see just one branch of a chestnut tree, and on the branch were two blossoms. "I often talk to this tree," she said to me…I asked her if the tree replied. "Yes." What did it say to her? She answered, "It said to me, 'I am here. I am here. I am life. Eternal life.'"

In that astonishing moment, Frankl touched on something profound. At the bleakest of moments, in even the darkest of places, we look for life. We want a promise of something better. We want to know that life goes on.

We crave hope.

Hope, however fleeting, was there in Auschwitz that morning. And, whether we realize it or not, hope is what has brought us together this afternoon.

In one sense, of course, we are remembering an event that seems hopeless—the agony and death of Jesus Christ. Today, in this liturgy, we re-read the story of His passion. We experience a deep and mournful absence—no consecration, no bells, no final blessing. The altar will be stripped.

For some people, it's still customary to turn off the radio, shut off the TV, draw the curtains...and pray. Some may light candles. Others may follow the Way of the Cross, or pray the Sorrowful Mysteries of the rosary.

The simple fact is: this can't be a day like any other. Scripture tells us that on the day Christ died, the world literally cracked open. The earth quaked. To this day, we cannot help but remember what was done for us. As the old spiritual tells us, it causes us to tremble.

But in the midst of all this, we do something remarkable.

We venerate the cross with a kiss.

I'm sure some outside our faith find it strange that we pay tribute to an instrument of death. But they don't see the cross the way we do. Maybe they should.

Maybe they should try to see that the cross was not an end, but a means to an end—the method God chose to remake the world. Maybe they should strive to see in the cross the beginning of our salvation. This is the wood of the cross, on which hung the savior of the world.

When the priest prays the Eucharistic Prayer for Reconciliation, which we hear so often during Lent, he invokes the cross powerfully, and poignantly. As the prayer puts it, Jesus "stretched out his arms between heaven and earth in the everlasting sign of Your covenant."

We are reminded today that it is a covenant that was sealed with nails, and splinters, and blood.

In the reading today from Isaiah, the prophet tells us about the suffering servant—foreshadowing Christ. Isaiah tells us: "He grew up like a sapling before him, like a shoot from the parched earth…it was our infirmities that he bore, our sufferings that he endured."

In Christ's cross, the wood we venerate and touch, we see part of the shoot from the parched earth. Nailed to this cross, he became one with it, and we are able to see this wood for what it truly is: a tree, like the one that prisoner saw, that holds out hope.

From within the four walls of our brokenness, behind the barbed wires of sin, we look out and look up—and we see this "tree" that symbolizes our salvation. This is how we know we are saved. This is how we know how much God loves us.

This afternoon, the cross speaks to us. It speaks of the one who suffered and died upon it.

It speaks to us in consolation. And—yes—in hope.

And quietly, but persistently, it offers us the promise of something better, beyond the prison wall.

"I am here. I am here. I am life. I am Eternal life."

EASTER SEASON

EASTER VIGIL

FR. PAUL HOLMES

GEN. 1:1-2:2, 22:1-18
EXOD. 14:15-15:1
ISA. 54:5-14, 55:1-11
BAR. 3:9-15, 32-4:4
EZEK. 36:16-17A, 18-28
ROM. 6:3-11
LUKE 24:1-12

"He is not here, but he has been raised."

Every story of the Resurrection contains the same critical elements. As they tell the central story of our faith, Matthew, Mark, Luke and John—all of them—report: One, that the tomb was empty; two, that the Resurrection took place in the early hours of Sunday morning; and three, that Mary Magdalene was the one who made the greatest discovery of all time!

Now, there's one more fact that's reported by all four evangelists in all four of the Gospel stories. And you might think it unimportant. They tell us that there were *angels* present. Luke tells us that the angels ask Mary Magdalene and the other women a question: "Why are you looking for the Living One among the dead?" In other words, "If you're looking for the Risen Jesus, you're looking in the wrong place!"

The angels are with us tonight, and I think they might just be asking *us* this question—or, at least, a question that's very similar. *Why do you and I tend to look for God in all the wrong places?*

We've gathered together on the holiest night of the year. We've blessed *fire!* But the fire we've blessed isn't the Lord; it only *leads* us to God. We'll be blessing water, too! But the water isn't God; it only *leads* us to Him. And in a few moments, we'll renew our baptismal promises. We'll be holding fire in our hands, and we'll feel water raining down on our heads. But those promises we make only stand as a *reminder* of God.

I think we're sophisticated enough to know all that. I think we probably know where to look for God—but it's what we *want* from him when we *find* him: Maybe *that's* the problem!

When someone we love is diagnosed with cancer, we know that God is close to us. But when we find Him—what do we want? We want *explanations*. When we're having trouble with our children or our parents, or our in-laws, or our boss, we know that Jesus is close to us. But when we find him—what do we want? We want *solutions*. When someone dies, we know that the Risen Lord is near. But when we find him—what do we end up asking for? We ask for *answers*.

But the Risen Lord doesn't provide answers to our questions, or solutions to our problems, or explanations about our suffering. The Risen Lord doesn't *provide* answers: he *is* the answer. The Risen Lord doesn't *provide* explanations: he *is* the explanation! And the Risen Lord doesn't *provide* solutions . . . simply because he *is* the solution!

We've certainly come looking for the Lord tonight, and we've come to the right place. We're here to celebrate the fact that we already *have* the answer; everything's been explained; and the solution is already in our grasp. Let *that* be the greatest gift of Easter this year.

That, as we renew our Baptismal promises, we remember that we've *truly found the Lord*—simply because we've stopped looking for him in all the wrong places.

ACTS 10:34A, 37-43	*"Your life is hidden with Christ in God."*
COL. 3:1-4	
JOHN 20:1-9	

Jesus and Satan were having an ongoing argument about who was better on the computer. They had been going at it for days, and God the Father was tired of hearing all of the bickering. Finally God said, "Cool it! I am going to set up a test that will run two hours and I will judge who does the better job."

So Satan and Jesus sat down at the keyboards and typed away. They worked Word. They excelled at Excel. They pounded out PowerPoint reports. They sent out e-mails with complicated attachments. They downloaded. They researched on the Web. They used Photoshop. But ten minutes before their time was up, lightening suddenly flashed across the sky, thunder clapped, the rain poured and, of course, the electricity went off.

Satan stared at his blank screen and screamed every curse word known in the underworld. Jesus just sighed. The electricity finally flickered back on and each of them restarted their computers. Satan started searching frantically and screamed, "It's gone! It's all gone! I lost everything when the power went off!"

Meanwhile, Jesus quietly started making .pdf files of the past two hours of diligent work. Satan observed this and became irate. "Wait! He cheated! How did he do it?"

God shrugged and said, "Satan, you of all fallen angels should know: Jesus saves."

Let me say something about 1) the truth that Jesus saves, 2) something about what the resurrection means, and 3) how we can believe it all.

Jesus saves us. From all sin. From all suffering. From all injustice. Wars and weapons, horrors and hate, torture and terror, fill the news. Teens commit suicide at alarming rates. Human trafficking ensnares young girls in 21st-century forms of abject slavery. The never ending revelations of priest sex abuse and the charges of bishops covering up the sins and crimes goes on and on. All the bad news....

And then there's the personal tragedies and sadness of our days. A parent dies of cancer. Corporate malfeasance eliminates your job. A baseball player realizes he'll never make the majors. And on a much more mundane level, it's another year when I didn't lose 25 lbs. during Lent!

Into all the bad news and failures of the world comes Jesus. Jesus saves! Jesus is risen! He is truly risen! Alleluia! We share in his resurrection. This is what we celebrate today. This is what we believe.

Easter Sunday a few years ago, the congregation was responding loudly and enthusiastically, "We do," to the renewal of our baptismal vows. As the last "We do" resounded through the church, a small, three year old girl, held in her Father's arms, let out with a perfectly timed "I don't." All present cracked up laughing. It was funny. But it raises the question, what do we believe about the resurrection? What does Jesus' resurrection mean for us?

Resurrection is not resuscitation or reanimation of a corpse. Resurrection is transformation. Resurrection is the promise of what will happen to those who die in Christ. Resurrection means "a complete transformation of the human being in his or her psychosomatic totality. Resurrection was thought of not as an event for the individual at death but as a corporate event. God would raise all the elect at the end of history" (*Harper's Bible Dictionary*).

The Son of God became what we are so we might become what God is (cf. CCC #460). That's not some Jesuit spin on theology. That's St. Athanasius in the fourth century. Jesus' resurrection gives us the grace, i.e., the power, we need to be able to live with God forever.

Richard Dawkins and Christopher Hitchens, today's militant atheists, have pushed their best-selling, but rather intellectually lightweight, polemical attacks on faith and religion. They say we are fools. Faith is ridiculous. Jesus died on the cross and that was it. Case closed. Death swallows us up in a meaningless, black void and we simply cease to exist.

Faith in the resurrection means we believe in life beyond this life, and that eternal life begins not when we die, but the moment we are baptized. We believe that the God who gives us existence, and preserves us alive all our days, will continue to give us the gift of life for all eternity. We know God has given us life now. Why would we assume God would stop giving us life when our bodies die? It seems to me that it makes more sense to hope for life beyond death. After all, I'm alive now, and that's quite a miracle.

Each of our cells holds some 20,000 different types of protein. That's some 100 million protein molecules in every one of our cells. There are some 20 million kilometers of DNA in the ten thousand trillion cells in our bodies. "Your heart must pump 75 gallons of blood an hour, 1,800 gallons every day, 657,000 gallons a year..." (Bryson, 2004, *A Short History of Nearly Everything*, Pp. 78, 399).

Every one of the trillions of cells in our bodies will replace themselves several times during our earthly life. So even though our bodies change, we continue to exist. Why should we assume that the power that has made us will stop making us after our present body dies? It seems more reasonable a bet to think the God who has created us will continue to grace us with existence in a marvelously new, and hopefully thinner, resurrected body.

Life eternal is not like a change of horses where we ride off into a far distant sunset on another stallion. Karl Rahner, the great Jesuit theologian, taught that the resurrection means we become all we could ever have been. All the limits of this life are lifted and we are all we could ever hope and desire to be (Rahner, 1967, "Comfort of Time," *Theological Investigations*, vol. III, p. 150).

According to Jesuit David Stanley, the resurrection means that the Kingdom of God has arrived on this earth. New Testament authors intimate that heaven means we join Jesus in his reign over the "course of world history. Heaven…is not a kind of perennial 'Old Folks Home.' It is not simply a place of retirement and celestial repose for senior citizens of the kingdom of God. Heaven consists in the active participation in the glorified Christ's direction of history" (Stanley, 1967, *A Modern Scriptural Approach to the Exercises*, Pp. 282-284).

Last year, a man who was essentially a second father to me died after a long bout with prostate cancer. Big Leo had withered away to a point where his adult children and I were taking turns providing hospice care to him. A few weeks later, a fishing buddy, Charlie, died. Another cancer victim.

I've been given the gift of faith. I believe I will see Leo and Charlie again. I believe we all will be transformed in Christ to live together in a "kingdom of truth and life, a kingdom of holiness and grace, a kingdom of justice love and peace" (Preface, Feast of Christ the King).

All of us have lost loved ones. Where are they? How are they? Rahner writes: "The great mistake of many people… is to imagine that those whom death has taken, leave us. They do not leave us. They remain! Where are they? In the darkness? Oh, no. It is we who are in darkness. We do not see them, but they see us. Their eyes radiant with glory, are fixed upon our eyes…Though invisible to us, our dead are not absent… They are living near us transfigured into light and power and love."

How can we believe this good news, this wonderful revelation of our God of love? Pray. Prayer reveals reality to us. Thomas Merton wrote, "Prayer is a real source of personal freedom in the midst of a world in which men are dominated by massive organizations and rigid institutions which seek only to exploit them for money and power. Far from being a source of alienation true religion in spirit is a liberating force that helps man to find himself in God" (*The Hidden Ground of Love* in Bochen, 2000, p.37).

Let's find ourselves in God, this God who loves us, this God who saves us. Let us pray.

ACTS 5:12-16

REV. 1:9-11A, 12-13, 17-19

JOHN 20:19-31

"My Lord and my God."

There's a Spanish proverb that fits Thomas to a "T": *Crea fama y acuéstate a dormir.* Establish your reputation and go to bed. In other words, once people believe something about you, you might as well go to bed, because there's nothing you can do to change it. Thomas had a moment of doubt—and for all time, that's how we remember him.

Look at Peter and Paul, though. It wasn't that way for them: Peter *denied* Christ—not once, not twice, but three times! And somehow, his reputation got totally rehabilitated. We don't call him 'Denying Peter,' do we? No: he's the Prince of the Apostles! And then there's St. Paul. In the Acts of the Apostles, we're told that in his younger days, when he was known as Saul, he used to persecute Christians. He was there when a crowd stoned the Church's first martyr, St. Stephen. And do we call him 'Stoning Paul' as a result? No. We call him the Apostle to the Gentiles!

Poor Thomas.

Thomas only speaks four lines in the whole New Testament, all of it recorded in John's Gospel: The first time we hear him speak, he says, "Let's all follow Jesus... so that we may *die* with Him." What a courageous thing to suggest! We might have called him 'Courageous Thomas,' because he was willing to *die* with Jesus. But we don't.

He then says, "Lord, we do not know where you are going, so how can we know the way?" And it was because of this "smart" question from Thomas that the Lord gets to say one of his most famous lines ever: "I am the way, and the truth, and the life." Surely, we should be calling this Apostle "Smart Thomas" for asking the best question in the whole New Testament!

The last words we hear from Thomas' lips are "My Lord and my God!" It's the culmination of John's entire Gospel. But why don't we therefore call him "Confessing Thomas?"

It's all because of that one sentence: "Unless I see in his hands the imprint of the nails, and put my finger into the place of the nails, and put my hand into his side, I will not believe." We call him "Doubting Thomas" because of that one moment of disbelief. And who could have blamed him? After all, Jesus was dead. He wasn't in a coma; he wasn't lying on a sick bed somewhere. Jesus was very, very dead—and he knew it. Dead and buried.

I think that, if you or I were in Thomas' position and our friends were in the grips of mass hysteria, claiming that someone who is very, very dead, and very, very buried, was alive, I think you and I would probably feel what he felt, and say what he said. But Thomas says and does something that is incredibly important. And it's not his doubting that we should remember.

It's the fact that he wanted to see the *wounds* that's so important. Jesus *needed* someone to point out his wounds. And if he didn't have Thomas, he would have had to find someone *else*, some other way, to show us his wounds. You see: Even in his resurrected body, Jesus had wounds. Even though suffering and death are in his past, his future contained the wounds he suffered.

Jesus was God. And he was on earth for thirty-three years. He then returned to heaven. Jesus wanted us to know that even in heaven, he has those wounds. Even today, God bears the wounds of the Crucifixion. Jesus needed a way to let us know that his becoming one of us was not just a short, unpleasant episode that's over and done with. No! God has a human body even now. And that human body, even in its Risen form, carries the wounds he suffered for our salvation.

Don't you see? Because of those wounds, *God can't ever forget what he did for us!* God can't pretend that it never happened. No matter how sinful we are. No matter how ungrateful. No matter how many wars, no matter how many inquisitions, no matter how many crusades—no matter what we do: those wounds are an eternal reminder of *how much God loves us.* Those wounds, even now, in heaven, are a reminder of *what God is willing to do* for you and for me—especially because we are sinners!

Those wounds are a sign of God's *mercy.* And if they had disappeared in the Resurrection, we might get to thinking that mercy had disappeared with them. No! Jesus *needed* Thomas. He needed Thomas' courage, his intelligence, his confession. He needed to show us his wounds and Thomas, thank God, insisted on seeing them.

And I, for one, refuse to call him Doubting Thomas. That's my story and I'm sticking to it! Alleluia!

Acts 5:27-32, 40-41
Rev. 5:11-14
John 21:1-19

"Cast the net over the right side of the boat."

My friend, Fr. Leonard Carrieri, who died in 2009 at the age of ninety-five, discovered at the age of fifty-four that he had talent in sculpture. Consequently, for almost forty years, he created religious art of great beauty and inspiration. In 2007, he asked me to commission him to create a statue. For "a story," he said, "that you like: Breakfast with Jesus on the Beach." I couldn't refuse him, even though I knew he was nearly blind at that time. I also knew, having seen him at work, that he saw very well with the touch of his loving hands. With help from others, his work was finished in 2009. And, on a Sunday in April, the congregation of the Sunday Mass walked in single file past it. Their glance was their blessing on Fr. Leonard's statue that he could hardly see. When I mentioned that Jesus looked very young, I was told by the artist that: "After the Resurrection, we all look our best."

Fr. Carrieri's creation in Sacred Heart Church in Camden, NJ, is a visual presentation of the gospel we share on the third Sunday of Easter. It is a scripture story, not in print, but in poured bronze, that rests in a setting of sand from Ocean City, NJ, with some seashells from there and some from the Sea of Galilee. These are from the shore that is thought to be the place where Jesus had breakfast after the Resurrection. But, in millions of churches around the world, this gospel will not be presented in bronze, but in a much better way. It will be proclaimed in the living breath-borne words of deacons or priests bringing the story of John, chapter 21, to the reverent ears of faith-filled women and men. It is a revelation.

In fact, the evangelist, John, opens the story with, "After this, Jesus revealed Himself." I don't know precisely what "after this" means. Maybe nothing. But, I know that Jesus was revealing himself after his death on the cross. It took place on a very bad Friday that turned out to be a Good Friday. (Regarding his burial, a piece of fiction indicates that people, family and friends, were angry with Joseph of Arimathea for giving away the "rock-hewn tomb in which no one had yet been buried" (Lk 23: 53) but embarrassed when they realized later that it was only needed for the weekend.)

Jesus revealed himself after his burial in that cave-grave with a big sealing stone in front of it. After the stone moved, and the dead body stirred in the darkness, the Light of the World walked into the dawn of an everlasting day. Christ is risen. Indeed, he is risen. Christos Voskresse. Vaistinu Voskresse. He "revealed himself to his disciples." The seven were privileged to be there. John, who was one of them, tells us that they were "at the Sea of Tiberius." Surprising it is, that he named the lake with the colonizing name of a Roman emperor. But, the disciples of Jesus knew this lake of Galilee by heart, and to it, they had returned after the stunning events of an awful weekend in Jerusalem, which is seventy-five miles away. The lake of Galilee—familiar locality for many disciples—was the location where Simon, son of John (Peter) and Andrew, James and John were called by Jesus. It was here that they cut the lifelines to family and livelihood to follow him. It was here that Jesus walked on the water and woke up to still a storm, and the miracle overwhelmed them. It was here on the land near the shore, that he fed five thousand people with five loaves and a few fish.

The Sea of Galilee was home, and Peter said, "I'm going fishing," where he often fished before. No wonder the others joined him. Night was no deterrent. They knew the place like the back of their hands. It was a long night. They were there at night on a lake that is the lowest level of fresh water in the world, eight hundred and fifty-three feet below sea level, "but that night they caught nothing." A letdown, surely, it was for them, at home in a way, with cautious hope after being through so much. None of them with too much to feel good about, the night of nothing was a good take on the way they were.

But soon the dawn that dared all darkness was standing on the shore, in the first light of the morning. They saw Jesus, and they didn't see him. He spoke (no recognition yet) and said, "Have you caught anything to eat?" To their "no," he suggested, "Cast the net over the right side of the boat." After struggling all night and nothing to show, it is amazing that they heeded this stranger's advice. But, it was a new day. It is wonderful, the way that God works with us, guiding us to do things that have greater outcomes around the bend of our journey. Thus, the disciples cast their net over the starboard side, the right side, as they were told, and brought up a miracle. The instructions had come from a voice that was three hundred feet away. The haul was huge. Too much in every way. A wondrous realization dawned on John. "It is the Lord," he said to Peter, who couldn't wait to see Jesus. He jumped into the water to get there first.

Fr. Carrieri's depiction of Breakfast on the Beach has one fish with a stick inserted in it, hanging above a fire. Jesus sits on a stone with a loaf of bread that he breaks in his hands. That's the scene the seven saw at the dawn of the day, and they heard Jesus say, "Bring some of the fish you just caught." A call it was, for them and for us, so that the "fruit of the earth and the work of human hands" might be part of a universal offering to God.

"Lord, I am not worthy," we say. The seven unworthy and uneasy disciples had storms in their souls like the Sea of Galilee. In his hour of greatest need, they slept when they should have watched. They all ran at the first sign of danger, and Peter, chosen to be the rock-solid one, waffled more than any. He cursed and he swore that he never knew Jesus. We all stand in that lousy line-up of desertion and denial at one level or another. How often we stand by the self, and not by Christ, who loves us, who suffered terribly and died torturously to save us from our sins.

But, now on the shore, at one of the lowest levels of land and lake on earth, there at a very low level of shame and regret, Jesus had three words for the seven, who sat with him at the last Supper they had, and then deserted him. Three words, "Come, have breakfast." Then, "they knew it was the Lord." After breakfast, Jesus singled out Peter and addressed him. Until this moment of individual focus, their eyes probably had not met in any deep connection, since the cock crowed after his denials, and "the Lord turned and looked at Peter." (Lk. 22:61) Amazingly, Jesus didn't use the name Peter, the name he had given him, but instead called him Simon, son of John, the name he had when Jesus first met him. Now, three separate times, using that name, Jesus asked him, "Do you love me?" It was radical surgery. Three times, he asked, one for each deeply wounding denial. By the third time, Peter was hurt "that he said to him a third time, 'Do you love me?'" One could almost feel the plea in his voice as he said, "Lord, you know everything; you know that I love you,' Jesus said, 'Feed my sheep.'" (Jn. 21:17)

So, Glory be to God, Peter is one changed man. He courageously tells the high priest, no less, and the Sanhedrin that, "The God of our ancestors raised Jesus, though you had him killed by hanging him on a tree." (First reading, Acts 5:30) Now, Peter is back on the rock, fearless and faithful. He would never waver again.

4TH SUNDAY OF EASTER

FR. RICHARD ROHR, O.F.M.

ACTS 13:14, 43-52
REV. 7:9, 14B-17
JOHN 10:27-30

"The Father and I are one."

*S*ometimes, *it seems, we can* hold on to an idea better if we can picture it or have an image. So I ask that you envision a cascading, descending unity that moves down, down, down, finally includes us, and then moves back up.

We have in this gospel the supreme statement of unity between Jesus and the Father. I and the Father are one. There are four clear unities in the Christian scriptures and this is the first one on which everything hangs and everything depends. First there is the union between Jesus and the Father. Then there is the union between us (our individual soul) and Jesus. He comes to bring to us that union that he experiences with the Father. Thirdly, there is the unity between Jesus and not just us, but everybody else. Whatever you do to one another you do to me or, as the gospel says, in relationship to the individual soul: what the Father has given me I now hand on to you.

So you can see the cascading unity coming down and then finally the unity between us and one another. You must love one another as you love me and how you love one another is how you love me. So John's letter says if anyone says he loves God and does not love his brother or sister he is a liar. Let me repeat it. If anyone says he loves God and does not love his brother or sister he is a liar because love is one.

It amazes me of the persistence of racism among Christians. That people who call themselves followers of Jesus still think there's a bit of difference in the eye of God between a black person or brown person or red person or a white person. That shows they have not even come to the first level of unity. I am afraid that this is what's destroying the world and Christians have not been any great exception at all. We have pretended to love God, but clearly for the most part have been as warlike and as racist as everybody else.

Rather, our work and the only work of religion is to create unity wherever you go. If you are not creating unity, you are part of the problem and you are certainly not one of the children of God. You can come to mass as much as you want and come to communion as often as you can. But you are not in communion. Our job is to live in radical communion and not just to ritualize it on Sunday, but to live it which allows us to overcome our racism, our classism, our homophobia, and all of our desires to make other groups inferior to ourselves.

Only that which is united can move back up. So picture descend - include, descend - include, descend - include. Always including more until everybody is included. So if the great unity descends from the unity between the Father and Jesus, Jesus comes to include us into that unity. Then as we work back up this visualization, only things that go back up are that which are united. Anything that is out of unity is not in union with itself, not in union with the neighbor and therefore cannot be in union with God. It becomes one giant image of unity.

Descend and include then transcend and include until finally you find yourself saying exactly what Jesus says, "I and the Father are one". The translation of the gospel that we hear at Church speaks of the Father handing over that unity to Jesus and Jesus handing over that unity to us and saying several times it cannot be taken away. The Jerusalem Bible that I study from has a different translation. It says you cannot steal them from me. Don't even try to take away this unity. Don't try to steal my sheep from me or me from God or don't try to steal yourselves from one another. For we see that any movement toward disunity is like divine thievery taking away from God what God owns, what God has a right to, what God is.

When we live outside of union, we have stolen from ourselves our own very deepest and best identity. There's a sad line in the first reading which you may have missed. Paul says to the people why do you judge yourselves and condemn yourselves as unworthy of eternal life. And the people respond by driving him out of the city. They don't want him. They judge themselves to be unworthy of eternal life. It's not that God judges them. They judge themselves. All judgment is in the human heart. It's we, ourselves, who reject this eternal promise of union with the soul and union with one another which is the only indication that we are in fact in union with God.

ACTS 14:21-27
REV. 21:1-5A
JOHN 13:31-35

"I give you a new commandment: love another."

This story is about two people—two very different people. They both attend a large suburban church. They don't know each other, and certainly wouldn't like each other if they did. But they sit in the same church, and on this one particular Sunday morning they listened to the preacher give the strangest sermon either had ever heard. As different as they are, they leave the church each Sunday morning acting so much the same that it is almost funny. Two people, very different, and one short sermon. One very short sermon.

Our first church attendee is a member of the church. In fact Earl has been a member for over forty years. He is retired now from his career as a researcher for General Foods. He has been retired about twelve years, though he hasn't loved every moment of that retirement. Earl is married to Elizabeth and they sit in the same pew every Sunday, on the preacher's right side about half-way back. They are as visible as church members can be, never missing an activity unless they are visiting children. Some would call them two pillars of the church.

Earl has served as an officer of the church many times. He has been on committees to help select a pastor, and he has supervised some fundraising for building projects. He has led many adult classes and taught Bible studies. Maybe the only thing he didn't do was get involved with the youth. Earl didn't understand the young people, and was always amazed at the people who tried to understand them. Other than the youth work, Earl had pretty much been involved in everything in the life of that church in New England.

It could easily be said that Earl and Elizabeth command a certain presence in the congregation. One might even say they were admired, if not looked up to. When the pastor is unable to be at a dinner, people always ask Earl to say the blessing. At meetings, he can always speak so well about the history of the church and the necessity of faith in Jesus Christ. The fourth grade Sunday School class invites Earl to come and speak to them about his journey of faith every year. It is almost youth work but he does pretty well.

Despite this pillar of faithfulness, this image of Earl in the church, there is another side of him that is not as well known. You could pick it up if you listened closely to some of his conversations. Elizabeth worries a lot about Earl actually. She worries about him because he really isn't very nice. In fact he can be downright nasty. Earl has such negative feelings about people, people who are different, and people in general. Sometimes he says the worst things. One day Elizabeth heard one of the grandchildren say to Earl, "Pop, why do you always have to use those names for people who are different. My teacher says that's wrong, you know." Elizabeth knew the names being referred to—she had heard them for so many years.

Yes, Earl has some harsh words for people and about people. You can imagine that he has some strong political opinions. And no one would know this, but Earl never gives to the mission budget of the church. He doesn't believe in sending money away. He just never trusts where it's going, and after all God helps those who help themselves. In forty years of giving to the church, he has never given anything that went beyond the walls of the church. Elizabeth worries about him, all right. He can be so stubborn, and so insistent that he is right all the time. He just doesn't care for other people very much. Maybe Elizabeth cares enough for both of them.

Up there in the choir loft is our second attendee in our story. She goes to church every Sunday, but she gets paid for it. Cindy is the paid soprano in the church choir. Although it is not her full-time occupation, she has been singing professionally since she graduated from college. The choir at this suburban church has a paid quartet, so Cindy enjoys the chance to continue her singing. Of course if she wasn't singing, and didn't get paid for it, she would never go to church.

Cindy is a social worker in the city. She works for the division of family services, mostly in cases of abuse or abandonment. She has only been there for four years, and already the work is exhausting. The caseload is overwhelming and the emotional drain is getting worse. Cindy's parents worry about her working in the city and getting burnt out at an early age. They ask her all the time if she plans on changing jobs. That's when Cindy goes on and on about how these kids need somebody to care for them and to love them, to look out for them. Some of them have no one except her. There is too much of a need to get out of social work now. Too many problems, too many people who need help. She has to do something.

Her parents are happy, though, that she is involved in a church. Cindy just shakes her head and thinks to herself that she is hardly involved. The choir sings in the balcony and she usually brings a Sunday morning paper to read during the sermon. Cindy doesn't believe in all this church stuff. She is somewhere between thinking that religion is a crutch and thinking the old argument about too many hypocrites. God is okay for her parents, but not for her, not now. She sees too much going on in the world to have anything to do with God. She doesn't see much "love of God" going on in the world. If it makes her folks happy, they can think she is involved in a church. It is one less thing to have to talk about with them.

Two people, Earl and Cindy. Two quite different people who attend the same church, and on this one Sunday morning they listened to the strangest sermon either had ever heard. It was a beautiful spring day. The church is full and the pastor stands up to get ready to deliver the sermon. Everyone is going through their pre-sermon routine, including Earl and Cindy. Cindy reaches for the front page of the newspaper, and Earl, Earl is crossing his legs and getting comfortable there on the end of the pew.

Then it was over, almost before it had began. The preacher had read her sermon text. A few verses from the 13th chapter of the gospel of John. "I give you a new commandment, that you love another. Just as I have loved you, you also should love one another. By this everyone will know that you are my disciples, if you have love for another."

She said a prayer and then started her sermon. "Just as I have loved you, you also should love another." And the preacher said "Amen". And she sat down. And it was all over. The congregation was quiet for a moment, then everybody buzzed a little bit. The organist played the first of the final hymn. The service was over by quarter of twelve.

Cindy left the church out the back, and Earl left out the front. They both said to themselves, "That's the strangest sermon I ever listened to….Well, at least we are out early. The line won't be so long at the Pancake House." They both listened to the same sermon and chances are neither of them heard a word of it.

> *"I give you a new commandment, that you love another. Just as I have loved you, you also should love one another. By this everyone will know that you are my disciples, if you have love for another."*

Acts 15:1-2, 22-29	*"Whoever loves me will keep my word."*
Rev. 21:10-14, 22-23	
John 14:23-29	

Franz Jägerstätter was an ordinary Austrian in the 1930's. Husband, father, farmer, and also sexton at his parish, he was a man of faith. Franz's life took an extraordinary turn against the backdrop of the annexing of Austria by Germany, the growth of Nazism, and ultimately World War II.

When drafted for military service, Franz sought the counsel of friends, relatives and clergy because he was morally opposed to what the Nazi party stood for. Those around Franz advised him that his service would indeed be compatible with his faith, but he could not accept that. Called to military service, he went, but was returned home. Subsequently he was recalled, but refused to take combat duty. Based on the convictions of his Catholic faith, he was a conscientious objector. Franz offered to do non-combat work, but the military leadership saw otherwise. Jägerstätter retained his conscience position, refusing combat service, and he was jailed for sedition. In 1943 he was beheaded as a final punishment. Franz Jägerstätter was beatified in 2007.

In today's Gospel from John, Jesus is preparing his followers for what is to come; these passages are called "the Last Supper discourses." Jesus offers these words: "Whoever loves me will keep my word, and my Father will love him, and we will come to Him and make our dwelling with Him."

He continues, saying that "the Advocate, the Holy Spirit" will be sent to teach them "everything." Jesus goes on, offering his "peace," making it clear that this is not just any peace, but something else entirely. Yes, Jesus says those words that we are all familiar with: "My peace I give to you." This is not peace, as the world gives peace or understands peace; this peace is the peace of Christ, and it is markedly different.

All of this might have been incomprehensible to the apostles at the table that night. As we know, in earlier verses from John's Gospel, there were questions about where Jesus was going to go, and worry about what would happen next. The apostles had yet to fully develop the understanding that the Resurrection would offer them, an understanding that, like our own today, will develop over time. Jesus was attempting to prepare them, even if they were confused by what they heard from him.

Jesus is seeking our obedience when he speaks about those who will "keep his word." How do we do that? Obedience is a tough go in our time, a word that can mean simply following the rules, or adhering to the law in practice alone. It can be easy to speak about those who are "rule-bound," as if they do not think for themselves. There is a different idea that "following the rules" earns us some kind of place of privilege. We can be a very confused people, can't we? The one real rule is to be obedient to Jesus! And in order to do this, we need to begin to attempt to live in his love and his peace.

Let's step back and remember our first reading, from the Acts of the Apostles. We hear about Paul and Barnabas trying to sort out the law in Antioch and dealing with confusion about the law in relation to Gentiles. Obedience is called for, but what about the adult male Gentiles? Should they be circumcised? This and other laws, as understood by the Jews of the first century, would have demanded a complete adherence, without exception. It is the teachings of Jesus that transform what the law means when understood through him. Ultimately the response of the apostles and presbyters in Jerusalem rests upon references to lives dedicated to Jesus Christ and the decision of the Holy Spirit. This is not about static law alone, but about love transformed through Christ.

Laws without love appear to contain a God who cannot and will not be contained. Our God is so un-contained that He does not stay "out there," but comes to us in human form, as Jesus. God as a baby is about as un-contained as you can get. The other side of this lack of containment is a God who in Jesus allows himself to be hung on a cross. This God demands obedience from us, however it is a far cry from strict adherence alone. This requires so much more, and it begins and ends with love.

An obedience that lacks love is not the obedience spoken of by Jesus. Jesus calls for our obedience, wants us to "keep his word." However, like the peace of Christ that John's Gospel reveals to us, this is not the obedience that the world knows. Obedience like this, and the peace that Jesus speaks of along with it, can come only from the Lord.

The promise of the Advocate, the Holy Spirit, stands before us as both invitation and challenge. The Spirit cannot be contained! Are we ready for this? The Spirit moves, and becomes our force for understanding, and for love. The Holy Spirit is how we are guided and inspired to express the obedience, and to live the peace, that we are called to by Jesus Christ. The revelation of God expressed through Jesus will transcend every boundary through the power of the Spirit. This will allow us to become truly obedient in love and in peace so that Jesus and his Father might make their "dwelling" in us.

Do you think that if Franz was present at the Last Supper, he might have understood it all? Who knows? But, this seemingly ordinary man did come to understand so much about the need to love and follow Jesus in a most authentic manner. He made difficult choices with extraordinary courage, choices that led him to certain death, but he made them anyway. It appears that he understood what it meant to keep the word of Christ and to follow obediently, as his conscience directed him to do, even in the face of execution.

This could not have been easy. It would have been easier to follow the local laws and just go along with what was happening. Even if it was incompatible with his faith, why not just "go along" and keep the life that he knew and loved with his family? Jesus never asks us to go along like that, though; Jesus asks us to live in the ways that he assures us, with the promise of the Father and the Holy Spirit, will always lead us to new life.

7ᵀᴴ SUNDAY OF EASTER

DEACON JIM KNIPPER

Acts 7:55-60
Rev. 22:12-14, 16-17, 20
John 17:20-26

"That they may be one, as we are one."

O*ur journey through this Easter* Season comes to the close as we gather on this last Sunday of Easter—for next week we will celebrate the great Feast of Pentecost. And as we pause and look back, these Sundays of Easter have acted as guideposts on our journey and have called us to be in relationship with our God. And yet, for many of us, our ability to see and hear God's presence in our lives can be lost—no different than it was for the early disciples right after the resurrection as they, too, experienced confusion, denial, pain and anger. But in looking back at these Sunday Gospels, our eyes are opened and we are comforted by the hand of God, the love of Christ, and the gift of the Holy Spirit.

For the past weeks since Easter we heard the stories of the appearance of the risen Christ. First in the upper room providing comfort and peace and assuring doubting Thomas. Then appearing on the shore of the Sea of Tiberias, feeding his disciples at the charcoal fire, forgiving Peter and reminding them of their calling to be fisher of all people. We then heard how the Father and the Son are one and that Christ is the shepherd who knows all of his sheep. The following week we were assured that everyone will know we are Disciples of Christ if we love others as Christ loves us. And then last week we were assured that we will never be alone as we will be recipients of the Holy Spirit who will teach us everything.

In short, the risen Christ forgives. He is one with the Father. He calls us to love each other. And he promises the gift of the Holy Spirit. All of which sets the stage for this final Sunday of Easter—where all three readings tie it together for us.

You may remember that we began our Easter Vigil with the opening lines of the Bible—the reading of creation from Genesis—and today, in our second reading from Revelation, we end our Easter Season with the closing lines of the Bible. We travelled from God creating us in God's likeness and image to His Son reminding us that He is the source of all life. He is the beginning and the end, and all that we ever need and want are found in Him. And that those who thirst, all those who hunger, all of us who are wandering are all called to come forward and to receive the gifts of the life-giving water.

The first reading from the Acts of the Apostles reminds us of how all of us are called, independent of our goodness. We listened to the passage of the stoning to death of the first martyr, Stephen, who was a deacon. So I take this a bit personally! Stephen was described as a man who was "full of the Holy Spirit, full of faith and full of wisdom."

His service as deacon was to the widows of the Hellenistic Jews. But for his teaching, he was stoned to death. And like Christ his final words were for forgiveness of those who were there. But did you notice who was standing there? None other than Saul, who consented to Stephen's death for teaching the word of Christ.

Saul was a top notch persecutor of the followers of Christ. In short, he was not a pleasant person. Yet we know that it is Saul whom God chooses to become the greatest disciple of Christ and who through conversion takes the name Paul. So this passage gives us an example of how God calls all of us to do His work. It doesn't matter if we are doing it right, or doing it wrong, or just not knowing how to do it. God uses all of us for God's work.

Which brings us to today's gospel—this poetic and rich passage from John. Since the 16th century, this 17th chapter of John has been called the High Priest Prayer. It is the final prayer Jesus says before his arrest and the words are directed to God. But this prayer is for all future disciples. And the prayer is for you and for me. It is not a prayer that asks for unity for us and God, but rather one that reminds us that we are already united with God and His Son. I in them, you in me. We are already spiritual, for Christ calls all of us his 'gifts' from God.

Fr. Richard Rohr once said that for the most part our thinking is backwards as it relates to spirituality. For we believe we were born human and are to spend our lives in trying to become spiritual. Where actually we are all born spiritual and it was God who sent us His Son so that we may learn how to become human: how to treat one another...how to forgive one another...how to love each other as Christ loved us. So, paradoxically, the more human we become, the more divine we become. Thus if you listen carefully to this Gospel it can actually open your eyes in a new way and turn your view of spirituality upside down as John describes this mutual indwelling each of us have with God: this divine dance of God and Christ and Spirit and us all being one.

The Jesuit Fr. James Martin just released his latest book, *The Jesuit Guide to Almost Everything (A Spirituality for Real Life)*. Early on in the book Martin talks about the various paths many walk to find God. Paths which are worn with those who have always believed in God. Those who believe in God and not religion. Those who reject God. Those coming back to God. And those whose path may be one that is simply confusing, or filled with bitterness or even anger towards God. But no matter what path we may be journeying, God loves us where we are, right now. In the words of the Indian Jesuit, Anthony De Mello, "You do not have to change for God to love you." The point he makes is that God meets you wherever you are—for God is part of you. God in you knows how to love you the way you are. Whether your life is like Stephen's or Saul's or somewhere in between!

Last weekend I was blessed to have baptized my great nephew who is 5 months old. It reminded me how precious babies are and how for their first year of life they are in this relationship with their parents that is all love, that is full of acceptance, where there is no need for anything to be earned by the child. But soon after, child rearing takes place in earnest and it becomes necessary for the child to learn hot versus cold, yes versus no, and so on. Soon formal education takes over and we are taught that in order to succeed in life one must study, achieve and gain merit.

The challenge is that many of us take this same model and translate it to our spiritual lives. We spend time focusing on what we feel we need to do in order to earn God's love. On what we need to do to make God happy with us. Whereas the model we should follow is the one we enjoyed in our first months of life. That is, that God is simply present to us, with us and in us—and there is nothing we need to do to earn it. Rather we just have to allow it to happen. We need to open our eyes to the fact that we already have what we often seek.

So as we bring an end to our Easter Season, here is the really good news about your relationship with God. Wherever you currently find yourself you do not have to wait until you have more time. You do not have to wait until your make your confirmation. You do not have to wait till the kids are grown. You do not have to wait until you start sinning less. You do not have to wait until you feel you can pray better. You do not have to wait for anything, or anyone.

God is ready now.

How about you?

Acts 1:1-11
Eph. 1:17-23
Luke 24:46-53

"You are witnesses of these things."

A hodgepodge of thoughts runs through my mind when I think of the Ascension, and this hodgepodge, I confess, makes for a dull homily: a little teaching, a little statistical information that you should know, a little challenge. That's it. But you've heard dull homilies before, so hunker down and put up with it. It will be short.

I start off by observing, considering how Jesus was treated the last week of his life, that he was probably happy to move on. Now he could take it easy, so to speak, and sit quietly at the right hand of the Father until Judgment Day. I think also of the nervous disciples asking if he's going to restore the kingdom soon, because this mismatched, less-than-perfect bunch are not sure they can hack it alone and, without Jesus, they might as well go home.

But then I reflect that the Ascension does not close the chapter on Jesus or his followers. Far from it.

Jesus' promise is that he not only actively continues to intercede for us, but also, through the gift of his Pentecostal Spirit, he lives in and among us, his disciples, in every age. After all, why else would he reply to Paul, stricken on the road to Damascus and asking the vision who are you, "I am Jesus whom you are persecuting"?

Jesus? He was dead and gone as far as Paul was concerned. But Paul soon learned that, in fact, in persecuting Jesus' followers, he was persecuting Jesus himself. There was a connection, a bond, an intimacy, an enduring presence. That's why Paul would later write to his converts and remind them that they are of the Body of Christ, such was the close unbreakable identity between Jesus and his followers.

This powerful presence of Jesus and his abiding Spirit reveal the fundamental reason why the church has endured throughout the centuries. It has survived, sometimes barely, the external onslaughts of emperors, kings, heretics, wars, famines, and diseases. It has survived its own internal corruptions, prejudices, sins, scandals, and misjudgments.

And today, as we well know, the church continues on its bumpy road. As you are well aware, it has shrunk to a pinpoint in secular Europe and is dwindling in South America where Pope Benedict XVI is trying to shore it up from the vast inroads of Pentecostalism. The church has lost considerable ground here in secular America where books on atheism flourish and where only twenty-six percent of us Catholics go to church regularly, Catholic marriages have fallen to half their usual numbers, baptisms are declining, and the youth, who are notoriously religiously illiterate, are drifting away.

But then, when I say that, some perspective is in order, namely, that you should know that we sixty-five million plus Catholics in the United States represent only six percent of the global Catholic population—did you know that?—we who always think that the whole world revolves around us and our needs. Which somewhat explains, by the way, why during the clergy sex abuse scandals, Rome was slow to act; it had the other ninety-four percent of the Catholic world to think about. Another statistic: Although we are only six percent of the Catholic world, we have twelve percent of the bishops in the Catholic Church. We do have a priest shortage here, but not a bishop shortage.

But the real truth you should absorb lies in this reality check: while Catholicism is losing ground in the northern hemisphere, it is flowering in the southern hemisphere of our globe. There is the future of the church in this millennium. There the church is thriving and growing in a wonderful way.

For example, listen to this: Africa went from a Catholic population of 1.9 million in 1900 to 130 million in 2000, a growth rate of over six thousand percent. Think about that. This is the most rapid expansion of Catholicism in a single continent in two thousand years of church history. How about this: Did you know that thirty-seven percent of all baptisms in Africa today are of adults? Contrast this to the average worldwide adult baptisms which are 13.2 percent. Yes, there, in the southern hemisphere, lies the future of the church which, in fact, until the Muslim onslaught in the sixth century, at one time had a glorious Catholic past and flourished as the home of St. Cyprian, St. Augustine, the desert fathers, and the monastic movement.

But what about us, where affluence and secularism have muted the presence of God in our part of the world? All is not yet entirely lost. History has shown us that, even in our worst moments, Jesus' ever-present Spirit can break through and raise up saints who turn things around and call us back to the gospel. That gives us hope.

A Francis of Assisi pops up out of the moral mess of the twelfth century. Maximilian Kolbe steps forward from the Nazi madness to die as a martyr. Thomas Merton emerges from the nihilism of Greenwich Village. Weary Rosa Parks says no to racial prejudice and refuses to move to the back of the bus. Nelson Mandela rejects apartheid and goes to prison for twenty-seven years.

Ascension and Pentecost tell us that God is still present, still speaks, still sends out disciples to make a difference, still calls, not just the Mertons and Kolbes and Parkses, but you and me. Jesus is here and still seeks witnesses. What he said in the gospel to his disciples on Ascension Day still remains valid and indispensable: "You are witnesses of these things." We should remember that.

If we do, it wouldn't be the first time in our long history that we arose from the ashes.

Taken from Once Upon a Gospel: Inspiring Homilies and Insightful Reflections *by William J. Bausch (New London, CT: Twenty-Third Publications), 2008.*

PENTECOST

FR. PAUL HOLMES

Acts 2:1-11
1 Cor. 12:3b-7, 12-13
John 20:19-23

"Receive the Holy Spirit."

We've all been taught that it's dangerous to play with fire.

When I was a little boy, no more than five, I found those kitchen matches. You know the kind: they're like little sticks, with big red tops, and they come in one of those 'slide' boxes, and you use the strip on the side of the box and you run the match over this long strip and the stick bursts into flame. It was mesmerizing! Especially to a five-year-old.

That box of matches was on the top shelf in the kitchen pantry. And I dragged a kitchen chair into the pantry, stood up on the chair seat, and pulled the box down. I don't know how many of those matches I struck into flame, but one of them must have landed on a pile of paper bags. And the whole pantry started to go up in flame. My mother got there just in time. She put out the pantry fire and when my sister and I refused to tell her who did it, she started a fire on our bottoms! I learned at a very early age how dangerous it is to play with fire!

Here on Pentecost Sunday, we remember how the Holy Spirit arrived as tongues of fire. No words. No explanations. No encouragement. No warnings. Just a roaring wind and tongues of fire. As with any fire, there was some possibility for danger. Not that the room would catch on fire.

But that this fire would somehow change the lives of those disciples. And change them radically, and forever. Before this fire, there was no Church. No sacraments. No preaching. Just Mary and a motley crew of cowering men, afraid of their own shadows, and afraid, most of all, that what had happened to Jesus on the cross was going to happen to them.

On this Pentecost Sunday, two thousand years later, the Holy Spirit may not come as tongues of fire. But the Spirit wants the *same kind* of transformation—this time, not in the Apostles, but in you and me. There's danger, though. As our parents taught us, it's *dangerous* to play with fire! If we let the Spirit in, the danger is that you and I might become an incredible source: of good, of justice, of truth and beauty, and everything that the Lord wants of his creation. The danger is that you and I might have to go up against the powerful forces of this world and make sure that the hungry are fed, and that the homeless are given shelter, and the sick and dying of this world are healed. But the real danger is that you and I might mistakenly believe that we have to do this alone. The Holy Spirit didn't come as wind and fire to just one apostle. The Holy Spirit came to all of them. Pentecost isn't a feast for loners. It's a feast for the whole Church—and we have an incredible opportunity this afternoon.

We can let the Spirit in. And we can let God's Spirit have its way with us. We know that it's dangerous to play with fire. But some dangers are good! *Little boys playing with fire in the kitchen pantry?* That's bad danger. *You and me playing with fire in the midst of the Church?* That's the kind of danger the world needs!

Let's invite the Spirit in! There's no telling what it will unleash in us, and in the world! Let's play with God's fire!

ORDINARY TIME

Isa. 62:1-5
1 Cor. 12:4-11
John 2:1-11

"You have kept the good wine until now."

Today, on this Second Sunday of Ordinary Time, we are invited through the Word of God to visit Cana of Galilee. In it, the great miracle occurred, the first public one that Jesus wrought. With it, he started his ministry to change the world.

Less than a month ago, we gathered on Christmas Day to celebrate the Incarnation, and for two Sundays since we have been celebrating glorious epiphanies of God in the world. First of all, the manifestation of God in the lovely form of baby flesh that was seen and felt and kissed. Wonder had a field day, as great events were celebrated and each one was a magnificent epiphany of God. The Marriage Feast of Cana is another one. Young John, the disciple, remembered this event, and he was the only gospel writer to save the story of what happened at the reception.

John would know very well that the themes of married love were constant in the Hebrew Bible, as God spoke in wedding-words that were very understandable to His people, from the sophisticated to the simple. God wanted to proclaim the tender, faithful love of His heart for His people. From the ache of creation, and the short honeymoon in Eden that soured so soon, to the sweet sounds of the Song of Songs, God often spoke in lover's language across the scrolls of salvation history.

It seems fitting that John, the disciple of love, more than any other, would set the event of a Wedding in Cana as the inaugurating moment of the public life of Jesus, whom he loved so much. A recent mural of the four evangelists, created by Othmar Carli for Sacred Heart Church in Camden, NJ, has John's right hand with the first and the fourth finger raised in the sign language for "I love you." It is a good sign anywhere. I am sure that John rejoiced in the words of Isaiah that are proclaimed to all of us today in our celebration on the Second Sunday of the year. Let us also rejoice in them. "For Jerusalem's sake I will not be quiet, until her vindication shines forth, like the dawn. For the Lord delights in you and makes your land His spouse. As a young man marries a virgin, your Builder shall marry you; and as a bridegroom rejoices in his bride, so shall your God rejoice in you." (Is. 62:1-5) And "you," of course, is us. God rejoices in us. We are called to a covenant of active Christian love of God and our neighbor. The poor, whom Jesus told us would be always with us, (Jn. 12:8) are a God-given yardstick to measure our love.

Sometimes our lives don't measure up and our presence in this world is like water at a wedding. No lift in it, no zip to it, it is flat, drooping and spirit-less. "I came that you may have life and have it more abundantly." (Jn. 10:10) But God invented need to be a divine dynamic, and in this story, it was Mary, the Holy Mother, who saw the embarrassment of the scene. And, she did something about it. So, Jesus changed the water into wine, feet washing water, if you don't mind. The English poet Richard Crashaw celebrates the Miracle of Cana with memorable words: "The conscious water saw its God and blushed." But, it was surely more than a blush that may only be skin deep. It was a total transformation. A delightful Epiphany in matter.

After the miracle, "the head waiter" (probably too good a title for this relative or neighbor, who stepped up to the plate and gave a hand at the wedding), had a good observation for the bridegroom, "You have kept the good wine till now." (Jn. 2:10) Most people would serve the best first. The poet Robert Browning has long encouraged young couples with this advice: "Grow old along with me, the best is yet to be," and John Greenleaf Whittier, celebrating "The Golden Wedding of Longwood," rejoices with these words: "Sweet has life's vintage been through all your pleasant past / Still at Cana's Marriage-Feast, the best wine is the last." However, not many can claim "all your pleasant past" to be true for them.

One day, several years ago, a couple of some Christian denomination came to the rectory door. They were old, interracial, and very poor. The man had come sometimes for food; she rarely came with him, because she was almost blind. This day, she asked me to say a blessing over them as a couple. Whatever vows they had, were made a long time ago, and seemingly were working.

So, I sat them down in the rectory chapel and proceeded to say that I would read the story of the Marriage Feast of Cana from the Bible. She piped up immediately and said, "I heard it before, years ago, in a church in Camden," but did not object to hearing it again. After the reading, I attempted to say a few words about it, including my favorite comment on it: "The wonderful thing about the story is this: there was no miracle until they got to the bottom of the barrel." I thought I was doing well, when she piped up again and said, "Can we have some food…some canned goods?" I fell head-first off my lofty metaphor.

Back on the ground, we prayed together that God's fullest blessing would come upon them. A big bag of food was quickly put together, and a vase of beautiful flowers was arranged. And then (it was a package deal) I took their picture, during which James made sure his kiss landed on her lips at the click of the taking. They felt blessed, I think, as they left. For good measure, there were flowers in her hands, and food in his, and one pair of working eyes to share between them. Poor as their situation was, it seemed in that moment, water was wine in their world.

But, there is always a cry from the bottom of the barrel, the bottom of the bare cupboard, the bottom of our hearts, the bottom of the world…a cry for transformation. We must do our bit, "fill those jars with water," for the maker of miracles. "Can we have some food?" she cried. O, let the bare rock be struck for clear, unpolluted water. Let the earth be changed from uncontaminated soil to wheat, to multitudinous fruits and vegetables to feed the hungry. Let the drab monotony of self-indulgent lives be changed into a wine of pure gladness and gratitude and generosity. "There were six stone water jars there… each holding twenty to thirty gallons, Jesus told them, 'Fill the jars with water.'" O God Almighty, let Cana be change, cosmic change, for the transformation of the world.

NEH. 8:2-4A, 5-6, 8-10
1 COR. 12:12-30
LUKE 1:1-4; 4:14-21

"Now you are Christ's body."

In today's epistle, written in the middle of the first century, St. Paul famously tells the people at Corinth that they are the Body of Christ.

Now hold that declaration in mind while I skip to the twenty-first century, to today. I'm quoting from a section in Newsweek magazine that is self-consciously listing the most influential people of the new year. Among them is a woman named Ingrid Mattson. She is a white Canadian Catholic woman who grew up attending daily Mass. Or, at least she used to be. She is still white and Canadian but she is not Catholic any longer. She is a convert to Islam and a professor at Hartford Seminary in Connecticut.

Her story is that at a certain point she no longer believed in the God they talked about in the Catholic Church. So she abandoned religion altogether until she met some kindly Muslims who led her to the mosque where she felt close to God. Then she says something as if grasping it for the first time. She says that she discovered that God was no longer in the church, but he was everywhere: in nature, in art, and in the welcoming faces other Muslims. She converted at twenty-three.

Where has she been? It was a remarkable thing for a former Catholic to say and one wonders what she learned from them, because, for all of its faults, the one thing the Catholic Church is famous for is its sacramentality. That is to say, its Catholic imagination. The Catholic Church has always been an extremely sensuous church, unlike other forms of Christianity which rejected art, wine, oil, candles, statues, stained-glass windows, incense, and the world. The Catholic Church has always held that the world is bursting with hidden signs of a gracious God.

Francis of Assisi was its spokesman when he sang of Brother Sun and Sister Moon. Joseph Mary Plunkett was its poet when he wrote:

> I see his blood upon the rose
> And in the stars the glory of his eyes.
> His body gleams amid eternal snows
> His tears fall from the sky.
> I see his face in every flower...

Or Jesuit poet, Gerard Manley Hopkins, who wrote:

> The world is charged with the grandeur of God.
> It will flame out, like shining from shook foil.

In other words, the church has always held that God is not confined to church buildings or churchy institutions. It is not the church's view that we live in a world devoid of divinity and come to church to find refuge from the world. On the contrary, in the church's eyes, our life, our holiness, our sanctity, our witness are to be found outside these walls, in the arena of our lives. Our sense of God's presence is to be found in our prayer, relationships, work well done, virtue in hostile places, and in the beauties of nature and art.

If this is so, why, then, do we go to church? The answer is that here in church, as an assembly, we get refocused, empowered, renewed, nourished, and fed in order to be the Body of Christ when we leave here. Here we are vitally reminded that we are more than the sum of our individual selves. Here we are reminded who we are, what we are: a People of God. With this knowledge reaffirmed, we are thus strengthened to return to our place of God-discovery and God-witness. With our sense of God's special presence here, we are ready to see his face in every flower there.

But there's one more thing, as Columbo would say, why we go to church. We go to church to be released from our self-delusions that we are the center of the universe, always a temptation. We are here to be challenged by the simple presence of others who are different from us and whom we are forced to rub shoulders with, whether we like them or not. Going to church, you see, is going to a place not of our choosing, to be with people not necessarily of our choosing, and breaking bread with people not of our choosing. In short, going to church keeps us humble, makes us realize we belong to more than those in our gated communities and that we are a part of a worldwide family past, present, and future. Being here reminds us that we are united with those in every corner of the world, from basilicas to barrios, from palaces to prisons, who, at this very moment, are celebrating Eucharist, and we are they and they are us. We are here as the Body of Christ. We are here to reaffirm this truth: No one travels to God alone.

This belief, you must realize, effectively undermines the popular slogan so commonly embraced today, "I am spiritual but not religious. I have no need of organized religion. I'm a player and move on a different plane." What a deception! It is a common conceit tailor-made for the "Me Generation" where the self is the sole measurement of existence. It sounds so "free." In this spiritual world there is no one to challenge you. "If it feels good, do it." In this spiritual world you don't have to sit with those "others." You can hang around with your own like-minded group.

In this spiritual world you are not beholden to anyone but yourself. In this spiritual world no one is going to point an accusing finger, because who can judge the self? In this spiritual world everyone's opinion or truth is as good as another's, so all is flattened out. Judgments and social actions are both unnecessary and arrogant. In this spiritual world no one is ever wrong—they're just in a different place—and, of course, consequently, no one is ever right either. In this spiritual world truth is what I believe it to be, morals are what I determine. In this spiritual world it's Me and God and I don't have to deal with that smelly person off the street who came in and knelt behind me and struck his breast and cried, "O God, be merciful to me, a sinner."

Religion for these "spiritual" players is too much work. After all, religion is pot-luck suppers and disciplines and dogmas and pews full of those other people. Spirituality travels lighter. It dabbles in the esoteric, in secrets hidden from those "others."

In this "I-am-spiritual-but-not-religious" world it's not St. Paul's insight that we are the Body of Christ. It's the self-serving slogan, "I am an army of one." But the church says no. There is no army of one. That's delusional and dangerous. Rather the church offers memories, traditions, links to ancient wisdom, and pits our lives against those of our contemporaries and predecessors in the faith. It demands communal living, understanding, and worship and gives challenge to our lives. As T.S. Eliot wrote:

> *Why should men love the church?*
> *Why should they love her laws?*
> *She tells them of life and death*
> *and all they would forget.*
> *She is tender where they would be hard*
> *and hard where they would like to be soft.*
> *She tells them of evil and sin*
> *and other unpleasant facts.*

Solo "spiritual" persons conveniently don't have to listen to that stuff.

We are the Body of Christ. We are here communally to celebrate Eucharist and gospel, to take courage from each other's presence and, thus braced, to be sent out—"Go, the Mass is ended"—with new eyes: to see the grandeur of God, to bring God to home, neighborhood, school, and workplace so that others too might see what we see; so that people looking at us might see what that former Catholic saw in those Muslims: that God is not confined to church. God is here in nature, in art, and in the welcoming faces of other Catholics.

Taken from Once Upon a Gospel: Inspiring Homilies and Insightful Reflections *by William J. Bausch (New London, CT: Twenty-Third Publications), 2008.*

JER. 1:4-5, 17-19
1 COR. 12:31-13:13
LUKE 4:21-30

*"Love is patient, love is kind.
Love never fails"*

"GTG." "BRB." "LOL." "ROFL." *Anyone* who's sent or received a text message knows what those mean. Last week, I read a story that put them in perspective

It was about a monologue, on radio, delivered by Adam Gopnik, a writer for the New Yorker. He said that he's learned to keep in touch with his 12-year-old son by sending instant messages back and forth. It's almost replaced ordinary conversation. He described sitting next to his son on the sofa in the living room, watching a hockey game, and the two of them didn't even talk. They just sent text messages back and forth.

Anyway: Gopnik's son, Luke, over time taught his dad the different abbreviations—"GTG" for got to go…"BRB" for be right back. And for a long time, his dad needed no help understanding the meaning of "LOL."

He just assumed it meant – logically – "Lots of love."

For the uninitiated: no. It means "laughing out loud."

Gopnik's son finally broke the news of what "LOL" really means. His father was a little embarrassed. But as he explained it, even miscommunication can bridge the divide between parent and child. They still end each day with a text message to one another. And they each end with those three letters: "LOL." Laughing out loud. And, of course, lots of love.

I think we sometimes don't understand the language of love—how to speak it, or give it, or receive it. And that is part of what Paul is talking about in his letter to the Corinthians.

This passage should be familiar. You hear it all the time at weddings. I know it was read at my own wedding. (It's one of the few things I remember from that day.) And it's even been used at funerals—most famously, perhaps, at the funeral for Princess Diana, where it was read by Tony Blair.

We hear it so much, we feel as if we know it.

But do we? Like love itself, this passage is often misunderstood, and misinterpreted.

The truth is that Paul wasn't writing about marriage, or romance. That was the farthest thing from his mind.

In the year 56, when Paul was writing, the church in Corinth was a mess. There was feuding and factions and finger-pointing. The early church was actually full of dissension and disagreement.

(I know: it's hard to believe that the church would have people who disagree about things. It sounds incredible. But it's true.)

Paul wrote this beautiful letter to tell them, in effect, grow up, you're missing that point! That isn't what it means to be a Christian! Being a Christian means, quite simply, to love.

Not physical love, not romantic love. But something that the Greeks called "agape." Sacrificial giving. Charity. That is the love Paul was describing.

And so he offers this blueprint for how to live that love.

Twenty years after Christ's death and resurrection, Paul, an itinerant tent-maker from Tarsus, crafts another kind of tent – the overarching idea that lies at the heart of the gospel. Something, like a tent, to shelter us, protect us, shade us.

It is love.

For love bears all things, hopes all things, endures all things.

It never fails.

Read that passage over and you realize: this is not only what it means to be Christian. This is what it means to be Christ. This is what it means to open your arms and bleed for another, and die for another. This is agape. This is love.

And yes, that kind of love also, I think, makes the best marriages. But too often, we think of married love as something else, something wrapped in white lace, clutching roses, while people throw rice.

Maybe.

But this morning, we are challenged to think of love the way Paul did, and the way Jesus did: a pouring out, an emptying of everything for another. For Christ, it wasn't lace and flowers. It was nails and thorns. It was a sacrifice beyond measure. It sounds impossible to give that much. And yet, even today, people do.

Friday, I got an e-mail from a deacon I know in Atlanta. He wanted to share with me some news.

Not long ago, he and his wife heard about an 18-month-old baby boy named Matthew. He was the grand-nephew of a friend of theirs, and he was born without kidney function. Two weeks ago, the deacon's wife, Marie, underwent surgery and donated her kidney to this little boy whom she barely knew and wasn't even related to.

That was remarkable enough. But there was another detail that the deacon wanted me to know about.

"The problem that caused Matthew to not have kidney function," he wrote, "was detected prior to his birth. The OB/GYN encouraged his mother to terminate the pregnancy. She refused."

The rest is history. Living history. Mother, and child, and Marie, the donor, are all doing well.

And now, Matthew lives. Because of this extraordinary act of generosity, this act of love, this agape.

Our culture, I think, has forgotten what love truly means. It's about giving yourself away. But we've forgotten that. We've become comfortable and complacent. We walk away.

We terminate what is inconvenient or difficult, whether it's a marriage or a pregnancy.

We don't realize what love entails.

But every now and then, you hear beautiful and challenging stories like Marie and Matthew, and the message comes through.

So, let's ask ourselves this week how we can love, and love better—not only those we know, but those we don't. Not only those we like, but those we dislike. I can think of quite a few of those—and standing here, right now, I don't think I'd want to give any of them a kidney.

But our faith calls us to something more. To be something more for the person next to you in the pew…or for the homeless and the hungry of Haiti…or for any among us who are hurting, or alone, or grieving, or angry.

So: don't consider this reading a romantic cliché, something that pops up at weddings or anniversaries.

Paul's letter to the Corinthians is for each of us. It is a gift. And one we are meant to pass on to others.

With LOL, of course: "lots of love."

Isa. 6:1-2a, 3-8 1 Cor. 15:1-11 Luke 5:1-11	*"They had caught a great number of fish and their nets were tearing"*

I leaned my head against the metal window of the bus. The soggy rice fields passed before the glass, and I wondered how the men, women, and children could work while keeping their hats balanced on their heads. Their strong backs bestowed them with exceptional grace. I imagined that it would be a good day of work, with the beauty of the hills surrounding them.

Then, as if traveling through time, bicycles filled the street and fields turned into grey concrete and metal factories. The workers changed jobs as we moved from rural to urban landscapes, from agricultural farmers to industrial workers.

I was fifteen, on a mission trip. There are a lot of question these days about the nature of these trips. Too often, American teenagers think that they are somehow saving people in other cultures, while people from other countries are just putting up with the oddities of our privilege.

I see the concerns, but I'm thankful that I had a chance to go overseas. My parents would have never allowed me to venture out of the country for a vacation or an educational trip, but for a mission trip they would. And so I slept in tents in a field in Switzerland, on pews in a houseboat in Hong Kong, and in clay huts in Africa. I traveled the world, under the guise of saving people.

Of course, as those things went, they were saving me. Each country gave me a different sense of proportion. It is one thing to sit in your cushy living room and see the images of little children with swarming flies and bloated bellies looking at you with big glassy eyes. You can turn the television off and walk away. You can allow the image to quickly fade. But it's an entirely different thing to be a college student, playing soccer with kids on a Tuesday afternoon. They show up without any shoes and you know that they have not eaten anything all day. Those friendly eyes keep their gaze as the inequities in our globe become quite clear.

The mission trips gave me the gift of proportion, even though I felt like my culture shock came with covetous whiplash—moving from want to revulsion. I had to fight becoming a complete social misfit. I sat with my friends as we compared the label of our designer jeans, scanned the pages of *Elle*, and assessed where we were on the fashion totem pole. I wanted the shiny products as much as my friends, even though I couldn't shake the memory of the family living on rice that they harvested from their small field.

Of course, it's easy to look back at my life as an American teen and point at my shallowness. Teenagers are particularly susceptible to marketing manipulation, and we allow corporations to relentlessly communicate to our adolescents how inept they are because of their lack of material goods. I was no exception.

But it didn't stop there. As we grew older, it wasn't only about the labels on our clothes, but about the car. Then it became about the position we held or the amount of power we could wield. It became about how well we married and what sort of real estate we acquired. We were still playing the same game, just with different prizes.

No walk of life seems to be immune to the comparisons. I once heard a colleague comment with great pretention about the company another pastor used to take his portrait photo. Ministers compare how big our steeples are, usually by assessing the size of our congregations, the value of the buildings, or the location of the church. When we meet each other, we ask benign questions as we assess our abundance compared to the next person.

In all of it, we become so sensitive to the manufactured needs that surround us until we are unable to grasp what we have. Even in our churches, we've lost our sense of abundance. We look at the budgets of past decades and see decline. We might even have an endowment, but all we can focus on is how much we lost. We look at our buildings, focus on the cracks, and dream about the next construction project. We become numb to the soaring artistry or acres of land. We simply echo that we do not have enough until our myths of scarcity become excuses for not feeding the hungry, sheltering the homeless, and working for the reign of God.

In each phase, in each walk of life, we become consumed by what we do not have and we lose the amazement of what God has given to us.

Yet, we can learn it again from the disciples who pulled up their nets and saw them bursting with shimmering, restless fish. They were *amazed* by what God had given them. When we pull up our nets, do we only see what we do not have? We've lost our astonishment, because we can only think, "We had more fish before the recession. Remember when the greatest generation filled our pews with *entire families*? We had so many more fish back then. Those were the days!"

The disciples remind us to live lives of astonished gratitude for all God has given to us. In the years to come, may we set aside our careful attention to our losses, and may we learn to be amazed with all that God has given to us.

To the glory of God our Creator, God our Liberator, and God our Sustainer. Amen.

JER. 17:5-8	*"The Kingdom of God*
1 COR. 15:12, 16-20	
LUKE 6:17, 20-26	*is yours."*

Twenty-five years ago, I read a 700-page novel by Stephen King called *The Talisman*. It was about a 12-year-old kid named Jack Sawyer.

Jack's mother is dying of cancer, and Jack wants to save her. He meets someone in an abandoned amusement park who invites him to drink a special potion, and now he's able to "flip" from this world to a "parallel" world that exists side-by-side with ours. That parallel world is very similar to ours—it contains the same people, and the same places—but it is also incredibly different. Evil people in this world are monsters in the "other world"—and Jack's ability to "flip" between both universes takes him on an incredible journey. In that "other" universe, there's a "talisman," a very special object with which, if Jack can only find it, he'll be able to save his dying mother. Those 700 pages tell the story of Jack's fantastic journey, "flipping" back and forth, from this world to the other, and back again.

You may be thinking that the idea of a parallel universe—one that's similar to our own, but very, very different—is the stuff of science fiction. And that only a master storyteller like Stephen King can dream it up. But I'm here to tell you, this morning, that we Christians already know about a "parallel universe"—one that's very similar to the world we live in, but incredibly different, too. And a real "master storyteller"—Jesus, our Savior—has already described it for us. And you've just heard a description of that world. Jesus calls it "The Kingdom."

In the Kingdom, everything's pretty much the same as the world we live in right now. You're there. I'm there. You're who you are, and I'm who I am—but there are incredible differences. In this world, the poor live terrible lives. And the hungry have no one to help them. In the Kingdom, the poor and the hungry are blessed, and it's the rich who are sent away with empty hands and empty stomachs. In this world, those who mourn are just what we'd expect them to be: devastated and sad and bereft of hope. But, in the Kingdom, those who mourn are happy. In the Kingdom, tears are turned into dancing.

I think our mistake over the last two thousand years has been in calling the Kingdom the "next" world, as if we mean, the world that comes "after" this one. When we think of this world as now, and the Kingdom as existing in some distant future, we can all too easily throw up our hands and say, "Well, I guess we have to wait until the end of time before the hungry are fed and the sorrowful are consoled."

I prefer not to think of the Kingdom as the "next" world. I think Jesus wants us to imagine that the Kingdom isn't some "time" in the future, but is a place, now, completely within our grasp.

I think that if we're going to call the Kingdom the next world, we should try to start imagining it as the world right next to us. It's much more like a "parallel" universe, existing side-by-side our own. And we can "flip" from this world to the Kingdom, and back again, much more easily than we think.

Jesus preached an incredible message. The Kingdom, he said, is already here. And in that world, the poor and the hungry, the sorrowful and the powerless, are all having a wonderful time! It may be invisible to us because we aren't doing much to make it visible. The more we feed the hungry, the more visible the Kingdom will be to us. The more we care for the poor, the more real the kingdom will be for us.

"Parallel" universes don't exist only in science fiction. You and I can take an incredible journey, flipping back and forth between "our" world and the Kingdom. Our passport for this journey is our baptism. And we've got one foot in the Kingdom already. To take this fantastic journey, we're going to need: a faith-fueled imagination, a heart full of compassion, a spirit-filled readiness to share with those less fortunate than ourselves.

We've got to start feeding the hungry today. We've got to start caring for the poor today. We've got to start consoling the sorrowful today. The Kingdom isn't the "next" world—unless we mean the world "right next to us."

Let's start making that Kingdom visible today.

1 Sam. 26:2, 7-9, 12-13,
22-23

1 Cor. 15:45-49

Luke 6:27-38

"The measure with which you measure will in return be measured out to you."

"*Love your enemies, do good* to those who hate you; turn the other cheek. If anyone takes your coat, give him your shirt also."

How often have you heard these words of Jesus explained away? Oh, well, see, these are ways to make other people look bad. These are sneaky ways to get back at someone. Giving the shirt along with the coat will expose the other person to ridicule for being heartless. Turning the other cheek is a way to defy and embarrass a soldier. Doing good to those who hate you will cause them to be shamed in the eyes of the community.

Those are all interesting ideas, but they don't really go with the rest of the passage. They don't really go with the last verse—"the measure you give will be the measure you get back." Jesus is not talking about "other people" here—that they will get their just desserts. He's talking to his own people about how to follow him. Even if this is not quite at the level of living or dying by the sword, shaming and being shamed still wield a lot of power in society. I just don't think Jesus would be recommending shaming others so that we might in turn receive a shaming.

But more importantly, these "explain away" ideas don't go with the essential Christian truth embedded in the middle of this passage, which is this: Be like God. Be holy as God is holy. Be children of God, who is kind to the ungrateful and the wicked.

Now there's one we really want to explain away. The verse that says God is kind to the ungrateful and the wicked. No, no, no, we cry! We don't like to hear about unqualified kindness! People are supposed to get what they deserve and deserve what they get. Now there's a verse we can get behind.

Except that Jesus says no such thing. Jesus says, God is kind to the ungrateful and the wicked, and we should be merciful because God is merciful.

Oh, how hard that is to hear and to accept.

For years, our family went to a corporate Christmas party, the kind with both a grown-up buffet (complete with grown-up drinks) and a children's buffet. People wore their holiday finery, and the children got to sit in a very kindly Santa's lap without standing in the long lines at the mall. Guests enjoyed lively music and entertainment and craft-making and lots of socializing. It was a lovely and fun party and our family always looked forward to it.

The invitation to the party always mentioned that we should bring an unwrapped gift, which would be distributed to deserving children.

Two things began to bother me about that last part, though, once I really looked at it. First, the passive voice. The gifts will be distributed. By whom?!? Or perhaps simply by conveyor belt? At any rate, out of sight. No relationship there. And second, that deserving children would receive them. Deserving children. Apparently, this qualification was added at some point to help all of us feel better about buying a gift and bringing it to the party. Don't worry, your Lego set or baby doll or basketball will be given (by whom?!?) to a child who deserves it, who will appreciate it, and not to a child who doesn't or won't. Your gift will not be given to a child who is ungrateful or naughty.

But your Father, God Most High, is kind to the ungrateful and the wicked. God does not distribute lumps of coal into the stockings of the undeserving at Christmastime. Might we consider following God's example instead of Santa's?

Now, it is true that bullies will be exposed as the bullies they are when we do not retaliate, when we refuse to respond in kind to meanness and brutality, when we practice non-violence (which is distinctly different from being passive or "rolling over"). But as Christians, our attitude about our actions and the source of our inspiration matters here. People may well be hoist by their own petard, as the saying goes, but that doesn't mean we ought to plan such outcomes with glee, as did Hamlet in the original context of that saying. Again, are we following Hamlet or God here? No, God Most High is kind. Even to the ungrateful and the wicked. We need to learn how to accept that.

And not only accept it but incorporate it into our own moral and ethical code. Not because we hope people will get what they deserve and deserve what they get, but because we know that none of us actually deserves anything. And yet God gives us everything, always. That's just the way God is, and because we are children of God, so too we ought to be giving and forgiving to everyone, whether they are grateful or nice, whether or not we think they deserve our kindness or our forgiveness or even our good will.

God's love is indiscriminate. That, in fact, is good news! Why should we be so bothered by it? God does not place qualifications on God's holy love, love that is not a feeling but a way of being, the basis of relationships (who is going to distribute those gifts?!?), the inspiration of God's and our own actions in the world in God's holy name.

Therefore, let us be kind, as God is kind, even to the ungrateful and the wicked. For we are indeed children of the Most High.

SIR. 27:4-7
1 COR. 15:54-58
LUKE 6:39-45

"For from the fullness of the heart the mouth speaks."

You can only lead another as far as you've been willing to go yourself. These words came home to me in a big way on a Confirmation Retreat that I led a few years ago. Toward the end of the course we took the youth away into the woods to have an initiation experience. On this occasion, we climbed a nearby mountain at dusk, where we built a fire and heard the story of Moses' reluctance to respond to God's call. I then led the twenty of us to a beautiful summit only a few hundred yards away to watch the stars appear in silence before hiking back down together. I had been there countless times led by others, but this time, leading the way myself, I took a wrong turn. Almost immediately we were lost in dense forest. As night continued to descend, the shadows over took us and we were, literally, the blind leading the blind. For what seemed like hours we were lost. Then, just as we were contemplating the challenges of having to spend a chilly night out, we stumbled upon the smoldering ashes of our earlier fire. I learned the hard way: if you're going to lead you better know the way!

Jesus put it simply: the blind shouldn't lead the blind. Still, we do it all the time. Our own actions and allegiances all too often reflect the values of a society diseased with war, violence, and extreme partisan rhetoric. These grave symptoms serve to show us how misguided we've become.

Luke reminds us, through Jesus' words, that the outcome is never good: we're bound to wind up in a ditch.

Jesus shows us another way. He shows us what true leadership is, and it's not what we typically think. Jesus has a way of turning the world on its head; it's another indication of how far ahead Jesus was (and is!). Remember, you can only lead as far as you're willing to go yourself. And Jesus was out there.

How else can you explain an expectation of blessing those who curse you or turning the other cheek when wronged? These are no small tasks, but they are things Jesus did and asked his followers to do. They forever challenge us. But isn't that the point? Being a Christian isn't easy. It so often comes with a cost. As Martin Luther King, Jr. said, "Freedom has always been an expensive thing." It demands something of us. In this case, that we grow up and become more like the one we say we follow.

I think it is safe to say that Jesus never requires more of us than he does of himself. We forget sometimes that he was fully human, too. He faced temptations; he felt hunger, sadness, and pain. He knew what it was to have to make a choice, and what it takes to exercise integrity in the moment between stimulus and response. He'd learned from life, as well as from instinct and study. He grew in wisdom and stature (Luke 2:52) to the point where he knew better, and was willing to tell us.

He did that not in a condescending way, but in an encouraging way, and not to hold us back, but to free us for living large. He knows what we're capable of and wants only the best for us and from us. Again, ironically, the way there surprises us.

Take the log out of your own eye so you can see clearly to take the speck out of your neighbor's. What's needed is for us to be honest with ourselves so that we can be honest with others. When we recognize our own imperfection we see others more accurately—not through the lens of their sinfulness, rather their goodness. He did that. Able to see the condition of others clearly, he could only act with compassion. He had mercy, he was forgiving, he understood, but he also knew that we bring so much of it on ourselves.

Jesus said, "Why do you call me Lord, Lord, and do not do what I tell you? (Luke 6:46)." Like us, it must have been so hard for his early followers to understand. And maybe understanding isn't really the hard part, following is. It's one thing to hear "don't judge," it's another thing not to do it. It's one thing to hear "'forgive your enemies," it's another to forgive them. So how did Jesus do it? How did he find the strength and the wherewithal to put his words into action, words that were consistent with his actions?

Perhaps herein lies the secret for us to become more Christ-like ourselves. I daresay that doing exactly what Jesus did is less important than being like Jesus was. Let me explain.

Any of us, from time to time, can muster up the willpower to stop judging, to forgive, or to turn the other cheek. Most of us have done one or all of these things at least once. But doing it once doesn't mean we'll be able to do it again tomorrow. Crash dieting is a good example: It works for a while, as long as our willpower is intact, but often results in greater binges down the road.

For lasting change to occur in our actions, *we've* got to change. We've got to grow into new skin—become more than we are right now. We've got to go further down the road, further than we've been before. We've got to follow Christ into a new life.

That's scary and daunting, I know, but required. Jesus said it like this: You must lose your life in order to find it and you must die in order to live. How did he do that himself? We rarely stop to think about it, but he did. He asked nothing of us he didn't ask of himself!

Of course we think of the cross, but it wasn't only then that he sacrificed for others and for the sake of greater good. If you really look at his life, he did it constantly. He was constantly giving himself away and so, conversely, finding himself. His desert experience may be the most profound example. Going into the wilderness following his baptism, he was readied for the difficult road ahead. He spent time in nature. He withdrew to pray. He studied the scriptures. He spoke to strangers. He touched the sick and no doubt was touched by them. He remained vulnerable to others. He lived simply. He had very little. He relied on others. He hung out with outcastes. He challenged the status quo. He loved. And most of all, he relied on God.

All these things helped to shape who he was and who he became. How could he not be forgiving? How could he not be patient? How could he not bear good fruit? It's who he was. And he invites us to be the same, to be like him.

For starters, we need only rely on him more than upon ourselves. He drew upon God's power and presence, as should we. To do so is to fill our hearts with good things, things that then have a chance of overflowing into our outward lives. Praying for those who trespass against us and blessing those who curse us requires our best selves, but also requires something more than we are capable of doing alone.

In her book, *The Hiding Place,* Corrie ten Boom tells the story of meeting, years later, the Nazi guard who stood at the shower room door in the recessing center at Ravensbruck, the German concentration camp where she and her sister were imprisoned during World Ward II. She recognizes him at a church service and she can't bring herself to shake his hand until she breathed a silent prayer: "Jesus… I cannot forgive him. Give me Your forgiveness."

Fortunately, we are not left alone in our becoming. God in Christ offers to help us, to enable us to say what we cannot say and do what we cannot do, to be and become what we cannot become by ourselves.

Leadership is something Jesus offers, not only through his words, but through his actions. He invites us to come along, to journey with him, to grow up alongside him. He calls us to grow into something more, the way he did. We're going to have to do that if we are able to not just hear his words, but to carry them out. He wasn't content for us to simply follow, he expected us to join him in the good work of loving and serving others (v. 40). At the heart of that is the invitation to come along and venture forth into the dark wood with Christ as our light.

1 KINGS 8:41-43
GAL. 1:1-2, 6-10
LUKE 7:1-10

"But say the word, and my servant will be healed."

Just say the word, and it will be done.

Just speak the word, Lord, and he will be healed. I know what kind of person you are and what kind of power you have.

And Jesus says, this is real faith. I never find people with this kind of faith among those who are supposed to have it. Instead, I find it in someone who is considered an outsider.

Most people I know struggle mightily with this idea. I know I do. Someone we know and love is so very ill, perhaps dying, and we beseech God to heal her. To bring him back to health. Just speak the word, Lord, I know you can heal her. Just turn your face toward him, Lord, and say the word, and it will be done.

And then the person dies, and we are left with the devastation. Why didn't God speak the word? Because we know God could. We know God can. And so did God simply not speak? And if God did not, was it because we didn't have enough faith? Did we not say the right words?

Well. We often say that God always heals but that healing may not look like what we thought it would. That wholeness may not come until we are gathered into the bosom of Abraham. And we point to the finitude of this body and this earthly life, to processes and the ravages of time and disease. I believe all that. I believe that healing is not about saying the right prayers or the right words or asking at the right time because healing is a property of God, a desire of God, a gift of God. It's not a transaction between us and God based on reciting the right words in the right order.

And yet....and yet, there are all these stories of Jesus healing people in the Bible—people he knows and loves (like Lazarus) and people he never even sees (like the centurion's slave). Jesus heals them with a word (Lazarus, come out!) or even without a word (the centurion's slave is simply found well again without Jesus having said anything). He heals them because they or someone who cares about them believes that Jesus has power over disease and death. And we want that healing for ourselves and for those we love.

And so we are left confused. Why didn't Jesus speak the word and heal my mother? Why weren't my prayers for my father answered? Is it because I don't have enough faith?

But here's the thing. Almost all of the stories in the New Testament are actually about Jesus. They are not about us. They are about the power of Jesus, the love of Jesus, the teachings of Jesus. They are about the character of Jesus, through whom we can know the character of God. But we tend to focus on ourselves as the recipients of that power and love and those teachings. We are tempted to make the stories about us instead of about who God is, which is also who Jesus is.

And this story says that Jesus is one who cares not whether someone is from the right tribe or is "clean" or "unclean." The centurion is a Gentile, thought to be outside the scope of God's care and concern. And yet this Gentile, too, is the recipient of God's abundant life-giving love and care. This story is a reminder (along with many others in the Bible) that it is one's faith and not one's heritage (or gender or socio-economic status or nationality or state of "purity") that brings one into the circle of God's friends. The evangelist Luke is telling this story to show how God works. Not only Jews, but also Gentiles—and, later in the chapter, not only men, but women—will benefit from Jesus' care. Jesus shows through his actions and interactions that nobody is outside the circle.

But the toothpaste is out of the tube for us about the relationship between physical healing and prayer. Even if we do manage to put our self-obsessed proclivities aside and read these verses focused on finding out more about who Jesus is and who God is, it is not long before we are tempted to apply them to ourselves and our own lives. And then we are back again to that question: why wasn't my prayer good enough?

Faith is not a once-experienced-and-I'm-done thing, though. We have to be converted over and over again. We have to repent (to turn back) again and again from our wandering away from God. We repeatedly have to turn back from our tendency toward reading Scripture to see ourselves in it instead of reading Scripture to see God and God's ways. We have to turn again and again from our tendency toward self-centeredness back to God-centeredness. We will all be healed and made whole by a word already spoken by God before we were even born. There is no trick to perform, no magic incantation to recite, no transaction to enter into with a bargain or a price.

And yes, that healing may not look like what we hoped it would look like. God may seem to remain silent in the face of our beseeching. It may look like physical death. Our prayers may seem not to be answered. But faith means that we believe that God has power over death and that love is as strong as death and that love is sometimes the only thing that heals any one at all.

And the Scriptures remind us again and again that love is there for anyone, regardless of their social status or nationality or religious tribe or purity status. Death happens, earthquakes and floods happen, bad things happen.

And when they happen, God is with us in the midst of our brokenheartedness. God crosses all barriers to be with us, crossing even the barrier of death. God is love, and love heals, and that's the last word.

1 KINGS 17:17-24
GAL 1:11-19
LUKE 7:11-17

"The Lord's heart went out to her and he said, 'Don't cry.'"

When life knocks me down and I realize I can do nothing of myself, I turn to Jesus like the widow did when her son was on the way to the grave. I hear Jesus whisper, "Don't cry." I close my eyes and pray the words he taught me to pray: "Our Father…" and my eyes pop open at the phrase, "Thy will be done." I remember: God's will for me is far more wonderful than anything I could ever think up myself.

I learned as a child to think that "God's will be done" means "accept the suffering that God has in store for you, it's for your own good." I'm learning as an adult that God doesn't want anyone to suffer and sooner or later "all shall be well, and all shall be well and all manner of thing shall be well" (Julian of Norwich). It may not be right away, and it may not be the way I imagine, but it will be, and it will be beautiful, assuring, and empty of woe and filled with peace. That is what God wants.

Mother Teresa tells the story of consoling a little girl who was sick and in pain. She told the child, "You should be happy that God sends you suffering because your sufferings are proof that God loves you very much. Your sufferings are kisses from Jesus."

"Then, Mother," said the girl, "please ask Jesus not to kiss me so much."

Mother Teresa got the joke on herself. How many times did we hear as a child (or have said as an adult), "God never gives us more suffering than we can handle?" As adults we begin to understand, the more we think that suffering is what we deserve, the more suffering we experience. Jesus came not to proclaim his Father's cruelty but his compassion. He became human to demonstrate there is not a way out of suffering but a way over it. "In this life you shall have tribulation," he told us, "but be of good cheer for I have overcome the world" (John 16:33). Jesus said this so we could understand that if he could transcend suffering, so could we, and if he could work miracles in other people's lives, he would work them in ours.

The way over trouble is to know that our Father wants only our good, not pain but joy, not illness but wholeness, not anguish but peace. Then, sooner or later, one way or another, we will be in for the surprise of a lifetime.

Whenever we pray "Thy will be done," we are surrendering to the truth that God is not a murderer but a giver of life, not a punisher but a river of mercy (Hosea 6:6). "God is Love" (1 John:4), and Love never wants to hurt us. Love can give only what love is. "God's will for us is good, pleasing and perfect (Romans 12:2)." In the book *A Course in Miracles*, Jesus tells us, "You do not ask for too much, you ask for far too little."

The prayer "Thy will be done" requires surrender, trust and patience. The miracle—unimaginable but inevitable—has been in the works since before our ancestors were born. It's happening before we even ask.

So when we are agonizing over what should be or should not be, it is helpful to be like the widow and put our fear in Jesus' hands. We can ask him for a miracle (God's choice of wonder) or our prayer can be this simple: "Please take these anxious thoughts away from me, Lord. Thy will be done, not mine. Please replace my thoughts with Your thoughts so that what I think is threatened or gone will be revealed as spiritual and eternal."

Few people have experienced a miracle like the widow's (some have) but it doesn't take effort for any of us to remember the many miracles where our fear of loss, real or imagined, dissolved like an icicle in sunlight. I remember many sleepless nights worrying about something I cherished like the widow did her son, and only when I couldn't take it anymore would I place my suffering, like Jesus did in the garden, on the altar of God's love. "God, I give You these thoughts. I can't take them anymore. Please give me Your thoughts. Thy will be done, on earth as it is in heaven." In the bible heaven is often a symbol for consciousness, and whenever I have sincerely prayed Jesus' prayer, God has replaced my worrisome thought with a forgiving one, and peace has replaced dread. Sooner or later, what was accomplished in heaven was manifest on earth, and almost never the way I would have plotted it.

It makes no difference if we have ever received a miracle like the widow's. Few of us have ever needed that one. A miracle is a miracle is a miracle. One is not greater or lesser than another. To God they are all easy. Let's say it now: "Thy will be done, Thy way."

2 SAM. 12:7-10, 13 GAL. 2:16, 19-21 LUKE 7:36-8:3	*"Her many sins have been forgiven."*

What a vivid scene! Jesus asks a critically important question in today's Gospel, and I wonder if anybody heard it. He asks his host, "Do you see this woman?" Simon apparently hadn't really seen her. We imagine her as a young and beautiful prostitute. Some even imagine that this is the story of Mary Magdalene. But it's not.

We're not even given her name. And Luke hardly tells us anything about her. What she looked like. How old she was. He doesn't even tell us what her sin was. And even though she was kneeling in plain sight, Simon didn't "see" her. *And maybe the centuries have made it next to impossible for us to see her, too.*

Who knows? She may have been old and her hair might have been gray. She may have had crooked teeth or no teeth at all. She may have had wrinkled skin, and eyes filmed over with cataracts. Maybe she wasn't a "loose" woman at all. Her sin might not have been sexual—it might have been being cruel and calculating and mean...she could have been a thief...she may have beaten her children mercilessly, or abandoned her husband and children altogether.

We're only told that she lets down her hair and intimately kisses the feet of our Savior. Our imaginations may view this as sexy and provocative. But that's because we don't know that a woman letting down her hair in public was a sign of grief. *In ancient times, women only let their hair down to let everyone know that they were in mourning.*

So why do I want you to really see this woman? It's because if we don't see her as she really was, we might miss the whole point of Luke's story. The whole point was that she was in grief over her sins—no matter what those sins may have been. If we're attracted to her only because we imagine she was beautiful or sexy or provocatively intimate—we'll miss the most important thing about her: *That she was in mourning for her sinfulness.*

Something, I'm afraid, *we* don't do enough of.

When was the last time you *wept* over your sins? When was the last time you shed even one tear over your lack of charity, your refusal to forgive, your impatience, your gossip? *This* is what Luke's story is supposed to make us feel. Not that Jesus forgave one more prostitute or one more "sinful" woman. But that this sinful woman was weeping in grief over her sins, and then weeping in joy over being forgiven.

I, for one, think we need to do a little more grieving, and a lot less patting ourselves on the back for not being prostitutes. And there's not going to be any real *joy* on this planet until more and more of us start weeping over our sins. I promise you: Tears of joy will come—as a wonderful gift from our Savior—but only after we try to really see the nameless, faceless woman in today's Gospel.

And then follow her example.

"Who do you say I am?"

Today's Gospel finds Jesus off praying with his disciples and asking them who the crowds are saying that he is. After hearing the various answers, Jesus cuts right to the chase and asks them, "But who do YOU say I am?" And it is no surprise that it is Peter that hits the nail on the head and says he is the Christ of God, the anointed one, the messiah, the savior.

But when we read the full answer Jesus gives—sounds like it is one of those good news/bad news replies, in as much that Jesus reveals to them that the Christ will suffer greatly, be rejected, will be killed and on the third day will rise. Then, if they are still on board with all this, they must deny themselves, take up their crosses to follow him. I am not sure if Peter and the disciples really knew what they were in for, but they knew who he was…they knew how much they loved him…and they were ready to follow him.

But that simple question Jesus asked his disciples is one that is still pondered by many to this day: Who is Jesus the Christ? Where do we see this face of God? And the question Jesus asked his disciples—Who do you say I am?—is asked of us more often that we may know.

Recently, I was reading a piece in the America magazine which told the story of the junior varsity girls softball team from Roncalli Catholic High

School in Indianapolis, and how the entire team stepped up to the plate when they recognized the face of Christ.

Their game was against Marshall Community, an ill-equipped inner city school who had never played softball before.

In less than two innings, Marshall had already walked nine players and Roncalli quickly recognized that they could easily dominate this game—but the girls realized that there was more to sports than crushing the opponent. Even though Roncalli had not lost a game in over two years they decided to forfeit the game rather than humiliate the Marshall girls.

But what happened next is even more amazing. The Roncalli girls spent the next two hours teaching and instructing the Marshal team how to play softball, instead of using that time to simply beat them on the field. They taught them how to throw, catch, run and bat. And as the afternoon progressed, and as the Marshal girls began to hit the ball—their faces lit up as they gave each other high fives!

Instead of another win for Roncalli, their loss became a win for everyone. Their ability to see the face of God in the faces of the Marshall girls allowed them to make a difference in so many lives.

And then, lastly, this past week I was invited to visit the fourth-graders at St. Paul's for an hour of "Ask the Deacon." They don't warn you about this in Deacon School. But I had a great time and was floored by the depth of some of the questions that were being asked. They started off with some easy ones like, "What did you give up in becoming a Deacon?"—Answer: a lot of free time! And…"Are you paid as a Deacon"—Answer: no!—and "Do you love being a Deacon?"—Answer: more than you know.

But after they warmed me up they started reaching down to some more detailed questions like, "When was the first Bible published in the world?"—answer: in 1456 by Gutenberg…but here in the United States it was not until 1663 by John Eliot and it was printed in the Algonquin language.

But after a few more questions, a bright and inquisitive girl raised her hand and asked, "What does the risen Christ look like?" In short, she asked a variation of the same question Christ asked, "Who do you say I am?"

And I paused, for I wasn't sure what to tell her. And with 25 pairs of eyes looking at me, and before I opened my lips, this is what went through my mind in an instant:

What does Christ look like?

Christ looks like the homeless person who we see on the streets.
Christ looks likes our brothers and sisters in our twin parish in Uganda.
Christ looks like the angry Catholic who is simply fed up.
Christ looks like the pregnant 17 year old trying to determine what to do, where to turn.
Christ looks like the gay couple coming to church.
Christ looks like the divorced Catholic waiting for an annulment.
Christ looks like the alcoholic and the addicted.
Christ looks like those that have been abused...and Christ looks like the abusers.
Christ looks like the elderly mom or dad in the nursing home.
Christ looks like your dying loved one who has just been anointed by a priest.
Christ looks like the baby who watches the face of the priest or deacon as they pour the baptismal waters over their head.
Christ looks like the teens as they are anointed with the Chrism Oil at Confirmation.
Christ looks like the faces of the couples who come before this altar to be married.
Christ looks like you and like me.

So how did I answer that question for that 4th grade class? I first asked them what the Bible says with regards to how God made us. And they were quick to reply that God made us in God's image and likeness. Perfect answer! (Kudos to the St. Paul's teachers.) Then I recalled for them the section from today's second reading—that we have clothed ourselves with Christ...we have put on Christ and thus Christ dwells within us.

So, while I am not sure if the leading theologians would agree with my final answer, I told the kids to go home and look at the face that they see in a mirror. That is what God looks like...that is what Christ looks like... that is the face of the person in which the Holy Spirit dwells. Our biggest challenge is in opening our eyes to recognize the Christ.

And so, over the next 21 weeks of Ordinary Time—during the summer and fall months when we will be with family, friends, coworkers and strangers...

May our eyes be opened to look for Christ in the faces we see each day...

May we be given the graces to carry our crosses as a follower of Christ...

May we recognize the face of God in the reflection we see in the mirror...

And may we be ready to one day face the risen Lord and answer the question we will all be asked: "Who do you say I am?"

1 KINGS 19:16B, 19-21
GAL. 5:1, 13-18
LUKE 9:51-62

"*No one who sets his hand to the plow and looks back is fit for the kingdom of Heaven.*"

None of the readings today are talking about the usual things we talk about. In fact, you may even wonder what they mean. Could it be because the actual things we tend to emphasize in the Church have almost nothing to do with what Jesus talked about? He's on a completely different level, as is Paul in his letter to the Galatians.

For in the second reading, Paul says, "For freedom, God has set you free and don't let anybody take away your freedom." Sounding like a relativist, he quotes Jesus by saying, "The entire law and all the prophets are summed up in: Love your neighbor as yourself." He says the law has no power over you, if you are led by the Spirit. Now, if I said that without quoting Saint Paul, some of you would send a letter to the bishop and say we've got a dangerous priest telling us that we can throw out the law if we're led by the Spirit. But those are Paul's words.

This shows us that we're not in the same ballpark. We're asking a completely different set of questions. Did you ever notice that most people when observing any denomination of religion ask, "What can you do or not do? What does your religion forbid? What does your religion require?" All because we spend our lives focused on obeying laws. Paul says it's not about obeying laws...it's about being led by the Spirit.

Now, that's not as simple as it sounds. To be led by the Spirit is not to be led by the ego, not to be led by your own selfishness, not to be led by your own self-interest - all of which Paul refers to as the flesh. Instead Paul sums up the entire law and the prophets by quoting Jesus directly, which he rarely does, by saying, "You must love your neighbor as yourself. Everything is summed up in that." And I think the reason we go through life emphasizing other things is because we really do not want to do that.

Let's be honest. Jesus never talked about birth control. Not once. Jesus never talked about gays or gay marriage. Not once. Jesus never even talked about abortion. Not once. The things we emphasize, and I'm not trying to make a point on any of those, are not the things he emphasized and that's why readings like today don't make a lot of sense to most of us.

We would rather do other things than love our neighbor as ourselves.

Just look at the typical attitudes of most Christians and Catholics toward immigrants. They tend to reflect the common consciousness of America, not considerably different than anybody else. We don't really love our neighbor as our self. Mexican or American? Gay or straight? Black or white? Based on our biases, we decide who we love. And if we look at the attitudes of most Christians, we are not any different. We have the same prejudices and the same biases everybody else does.

We do not love our neighbor as our self. It's much easier to just kick around the poor like everybody else does. Most recently, many people opposed healthcare reform because they didn't want the poor getting a bit more of their money. Yet you can hardly go through two paragraphs of the New Testament without Jesus telling us to love the poor. Are we really a nation that loves the poor? Are we really different because of the gospel? Is it really an entirely different framework through which we read reality and read the moment?

If you doubt that, reread today's gospel. This doesn't sound like the way we think. A guy asks, "Can I go and bury my father first?" Jesus says, "No, let the dead bury the dead." Now, if I said that you'd also write a letter to the bishop. Those of you who are old enough perhaps remember before Vatican II that the majority of the time the priest wore black vestments at mass. The great Church had largely become a funereal society of requiem masses saving the souls in Purgatory. Despite the fact that Jesus reminded us that religion is about the living, not the dead. But culture gets preoccupied with those who are gone instead of those who are here and, in turn, we reflect the same thing.

Jesus forewarned us when he basically said, "Foxes have dens, birds have nests, but the human one has nowhere to lay his head. If you follow me you're not gonna fit in any usual camp. The liberals don't make sense to you and the conservatives don't make sense to you. You're lost in the middle. You have nowhere to lay your head." He then ends it using a passage that Saint Francis actually quotes in our Franciscan Rule: "No one who sets his hand to the plow and looks back is fit for the kingdom of Heaven." My gosh.

But as I look at the world, in so many countries that I've taught in, you see that most people keep reliving the past over and over and over and over again. And most of the wars and hatreds and genocides are people who just keep looking back and keep replaying what was done to their ancestors centuries ago. That's why Jesus said, "Anybody who looks back is not fit for the kingdom of God." You've got to live right now. Either God and the gospel and grace are available to us right now or we don't get it.

But most of us reflect the biases, the hurts, the agendas, and the fears of the past that we live over and over again. That is what Paul calls, in the second reading, slavery. There is no inner freedom. There is no inner life. There is a lack of grace to see the moment as the moment. You decide who is in and who is out. Who you like and who you do not like. Who is legal and who is illegal. But in the kingdom of God, all people are equal. And the kingdom of God is all the world. So when you start deciding that certain groups are undesirable or illegal then you're not a kingdom person. You're much more an American than you are a Christian. And despite reading these gospels Sunday after Sunday, we have remained satisfied with that kind of Christianity

I wonder what most priests are preaching about after they read such a gospel as this. For either the gospel changes the world, changes your mind, or it's not the gospel. Either it creates good news for the poor, as Jesus first put it, or in fact, it's not good news at all.

Isa. 66:10-14c
Gal. 6:14-18
Luke 10:1-12, 17-20

"Rejoice because your names are written in heaven."

In the ancient biblical world, it was believed that there were just seventy-two nations. That is, if you count all the descendants of Noah's three sons—Shem, Ham, and Japeth—you come up with seventy-two, the only survivors of the flood and therefore the ancestors of the human race. So the number seventy-two came to represent all the nations. Thus in his gospel Luke is saying that in choosing the seventy-two Jesus is sending his disciples not only to Israel, but to the whole world.

So, as we heard, he sends them out two by two, just like the Mormons and Jehovah Witnesses, who knock at our doors. Speaking of which, one humorist says one day he was late leaving home for work when there was a knock at his front door. It was wet and cold outside. He opened the door and there were two Jehovah Witnesses damp and shivering in the cold. They asked if they could come inside. Well, he just couldn't just leave them standing there, so he said okay. He brought them into his living room and offered them a chair. They were quiet for a long time, so he asked, "What happens now?" The older one said, "We don't know. We never got this far before."

Anyway, as you heard, the disciples came back jubilant at their success but they were caught up short when Jesus told them not to be so happy that spirits were subject to them, but rather because their names were written in heaven. That is to say, they should rejoice because they made a difference to someone beyond themselves, they were part of something larger.

And that, in the most profound sense, is the Christian formula for success. Make a moral difference, be a part of something larger. It's a simple teaching and yet it is as far as you can get from the world's criteria of success, which is having for oneself lots of money, position, consuming a lot, being a celebrity, an army of one. Forget the Band of Brothers.

Yet, when it is tried....I know a man who is a member of what we call today the "Greatest Generation." He served in World War II, was in the Normandy invasion and D Day. He tells me of the sufferings, the deprivation, the horror of the war. But then he always says, "Still, I look back on those four years as the very best years of my life. For once in my life I really had the feeling that I was part of something bigger than myself. I was on the move. We had a mission. Maybe it's sad to say, but I look back upon those years as the best of my life."

Notice what he said. The best part of his life was when he was "part of something bigger...we had a mission." Today when so many measure everything by something smaller—that is, themselves, their needs, their wants; when any sense of what is best for the common good is simply not on their mental radar; when education and advertising are geared toward "the good life," which means one of endless self-fulfillment—few lives are successful in the gospel sense, in the human sense.

To be currently specific: the people who made millions in the Oil-for-Food scandal at the United Nations; money stolen from the poor people of Iraq; corruption at the World Bank; the 210-million-dollar separation package given to the head of Home Depot, who was fired for doing a poor job; and the other thirty-six chief executives ousted last year who walked away with over a billion dollars among them; public officials routinely convicted of corruption; Congress wallowing in shameless earmarks and lobbyists' money. Did you know that there were sixty-two lobbyists in 1968 but that today there more than 15,000 of them, including some 2400 former public officials and some 240 ex-members of Congress? The pharmaceutical lobby, for example, has two lobbyists for each of the 535 member of Congress.

University officials steering unsuspecting students into taking loans from banks in which they have a financial interest, doctors pushing drugs from companies from which they have received extravagant perks and gifts, the obsessive idolatry of high self-centered consumers like Paris Hilton—all these high salaried, high-positioned people are not only mired in irresistible greed but, gospel-wise, they reveal themselves as morally incapable of purpose or any sense of the common good. Yet, by the world's standards, they are considered "successful."

That's why it's troubling that, according to the Los Angeles Times, a new study indicates that young adults today are more narcissistic and ego-driven than the previous generation. Some suggest causes such as permissive parenting, increased materialism, the fascination with celebrities. Certainly there's the almost total immersion in the self-centered world of cell phones, iPods, BlackBerrys, iPhones, and other solitary electronic games making a new generation decidedly less interested in giving their time to others or being a part of something larger and, who, therefore, quotes the report, "tend to have less interest in emotionally intimate bonds."

I remember a college girl telling me that, unlike her sister who went a few years ago, she definitely was not going this year with us on our parish-sponsored Jesuit Volunteer Program to work in a poor country. "Why?" I asked. She said, "Because Jane went with you to Honduras and it totally destroyed her life. When she came back she wasn't the same person. She changed the course of her life and upset everybody."

Well, that was the best reason I ever heard for actually going. Jane did drop out of the me-alone generation and wanted to do something with her life and become a part of something larger. Yet Jane's attitude should be a normal part of being a Christian, not a cause for concern.

Anyway, to test your spirituality, ask yourself: How passionate am I to make a moral difference with my life? Does the common good figure in my decisions or only "What's in it for me and mine?" If someone remarks that you are "successful," what do they mean? Money, big house, exotic vacations, prestigious job, promotions, upscale neighborhood, three cars?

Would you be defined as successful in terms of your consumption or in terms of your life, that it matters, really matters in the good that you do, the time you give, the care, concern, and compassion you show for others? Has your life at this stage transcended itself and become a part of something bigger, grander, than your needs? Have you a sense of mission, of being chosen and sent?

This gospel raises these very questions and so, as usual, it turns out to be more subversive than we think. "Rejoice that your names are written in heaven."

Taken from Once Upon a Gospel: Inspiring Homilies and Insightful Reflections *by William J. Bausch (New London, CT: Twenty-Third Publications), 2008.*

15ᵀᴴ SUNDAY IN ORDINARY TIME

MICHAEL DOYLE

Dᴇᴜᴛ. 30:10-14
Cᴏʟ. 1:15-20
Lᴜᴋᴇ 10: 25-37

"Go and do likewise."

S everal years ago, I was taken by car from Jerusalem to Jericho. It didn't take long. It's only seventeen miles. What I remember most vividly was a road sign I had not seen anywhere before: "Passing sea level." There and then, my mind went to the word "down" in the story Jesus told about the Good Samaritan. "There was a man going down from Jerusalem to Jericho." (Lk.10:30) Going down, he surely was. I didn't know then that Jerusalem ascends suddenly to an altitude of two thousand feet above the land nearby, and Jericho descends to eight hundred and fifty-three feet below the sea. The road between the two cities does not descend as a straight and narrow path, but in a winding, dangerous, downward pattern.

In another sense, straight and narrow would seem to describe "the scholar of the law who stood up," not to greet Jesus or acknowledge him, but "to test him," by saying, "Teacher, what must I do to inherit eternal life?" (Lk.10:25) Details of law were big in this man's mind. There is no way he could as yet accept that "God is love." He would defend the case till he dropped that the thief on his cross beside Jesus, sentenced to be executed for his crimes, should not get eternal life. But he did. In this situation, Jesus, not wanting to argue, answered the question with a question: "What is written in the law?" The lawyer knew the law and said, "You shall love the Lord, your God, with all your heart, with all your being, with all your strength, and with all your mind, and your neighbor as yourself." (Lk.10:27) It was a correct answer, surely. And Jesus said, "Do this and you will live." The lawyer's test of Jesus had not gone well. He found himself answering his own question, and then, wishing to justify himself, he said to Jesus, "and who is my neighbor?"

With that question, the lawyer opened a bulky bag, not of worms, but of birds that flew out in countless directions and would never go back into the bag. There is no legal answer to that question, then or now. So Jesus responded with a story, a great story: The Good Samaritan. "A man went down from Jerusalem to Jericho and fell among robbers. They stripped him and beat him and left him half dead." (Lk.10:30) Shortly afterwards, a priest, upright as the law-teacher, came along and saw the beaten man, but walked by on the opposite side of the road. One has to be careful, he thought. It might be a trap. In a modern version, he might be an illegal immigrant, a drug addict, an alcoholic, some useless, homeless character. In my position, the priest thought, I don't associate with "them." I am a law-abiding citizen. Then, a Levite came and he also thought that in his position, it is not appropriate to associate with certain types. This fellow lying along the road is probably a robber, too. He double-crossed his gang, and they got him. If he was upright and worked hard, this wouldn't happen to him. Finally, the man from Samaria came, one of "them" Samaritans. People avoid them. They are half breeds…not like us at all. We don't go there, we keep our distance, and we wouldn't ever want them in our neighborhood. We paid good money for our houses. We don't want any of them hurting our real estate values. It is not good for the economy.

But, in the story that Jesus told, it was one of "them" who came along on the road to Jericho. Unlike the priest and the Levite, "He was moved with compassion at the sight. He approached him and dressed his wounds and brought him to an inn where he cared for him. The next day, he took out two silver pieces and gave them to the inn keeper with the request, 'Look after him.'" (Lk.10:33-35)

Now Jesus had a question for the lawyer and for all of us. "Which of these three, in your opinion, was neighbor to the man who fell among the robbers?" The lawyer had proclaimed what he stood for, and it was "what is written in the law." Love God fully and "your neighbor as yourself." Then the question: Who was neighbor in this case? He was forced to dismiss the upright of his society and choose over them, the lowly Samaritan. "The one who treated him with compassion," he said. (Lk.10:37) He treated him well. This Samaritan was good because he had a heart of compassion. He wasn't heartless like the other two. He knew in his heart what to do.

Moses, in the first reading, tells us that God's command "is not up in the sky," up in the air. "No, it is something very near to you...already in your hearts." (Dt. 30: 12-14)

It was already in the humble heart of this Samaritan, what he should do. He didn't need to know the race, nationality, tribal identity, occupation, or financial status of the beaten, bloodied man on the roadside. One thing for sure, he knew he wasn't a Samaritan. He gave no thought to such things. "He approached the victim and poured oil and wine over his wounds and bandaged them." (Lk.10:34) Those bandages stretched over old wounds of hatred and prejudice that needed healing and still do. Reconciliation is always the aching plea of God along the long, bloody highway of human history, and opportunities for it often show up around the bend of the road.

A white woman I have known for many years was on her first visit to a friend who was very ill in Jefferson Hospital in Philadelphia. Not realizing that the cost of meter-parking had doubled, she put in her four quarters and got less than half an hour, which was not enough. Disappointed, she moved on, and for some reason, turned and saw an African American man putting quarters in her meter. She thanked him, and thinking that she would get change in the hospital store to repay him after the visit, she said, "Will you be here when I come back?" She wasn't prepared for his response. "I will," he said, "I live here." She followed his gaze and there was the large, cardboard box. He was a homeless man. It was a moment of inestimable respect, gratitude, and healing.

Looking at the world today, as men and women have looked at it in every age, we can be overwhelmed by the seeming impenetrable walls of hate and prejudice that exist between human beings. Nevertheless, we have a daring hope that will not be denied.

The second reading for this Fifteenth Sunday of the Year has lines from the letter of Paul to the Colossians, that will always sustain that hope. "Christ Jesus is the image of the invisible God, the first born of all creatures. In him everything in heaven and on earth was created. In him, everything continues in being. It pleased God to make absolute fullness reside in him and by means, to reconcile everything in his person, everything, I say, both on earth and in the heavens, making peace through the blood of his cross." (Col.1:15-20)

O, God be praised for sending your Son to take on the division and abuse and violence of the human race. He didn't use a study or a survey or a strategy of penalty and isolation. His approach is not to scrape out the badness with the steel wool of legal enforcement. No. He set out to absorb the corruption in the cotton wool of himself. We must do our bit to absorb it, too.

Paul tells us, "In my body I am filling up what is wanting in the sufferings of Christ, on behalf of his body, which is the Church." (Col.1:24)

Every day, in numbers uncountable, people are risking and reaching through the barbed wire of division to heal others and add their effort to the healing, to the essence of Christ's mission of "reconciling everything in his person, making peace through the blood of his cross."

GEN. 18:1-10A
COL. 1:24-28
LUKE 10:38-42

"Mary has chosen the better part and it will not be taken from her."

I don't know about you, but when I was growing up this Gospel used to irk me. Here we find Martha busting her back to get the food ready and to serve the guests who have gathered in her home while her sister, Mary, is chilling out listening to Jesus teach. And when Martha says something to Jesus—OK, actually it sounds more like she was whining to Jesus—he defends Mary's decision of opting out of the work. And for those of us who are type A and love to run around doing things, it has us wondering what this is all about!

But actually, if we take a moment to step back and reflect a bit and add in some 1st-century context, we can begin to see what the core message of this Gospel is and how it can speak to us today. It is interesting to note that during this summer month of July, when we are spending time on vacation, visiting family and friends, that the Church provides us these series of Gospels centered on the tenth chapter of Luke. In some respect you could call this the month of Discipleship, as the gospels of the four Sundays of July provide us the guidelines of what we are called to do as baptized Christians.

The month started out with the beginning of Luke's tenth chapter, when Christ appoints and sends 72 disciples out to do his work. He warns them the road will not always be easy and that they will not always be accepted. But they were asked to drop everything and go bring peace to households. With this we, too, are reminded that our baptism calls us to do the same and minister to those that we meet, knowing that the journey will not always be easy. Then, last week, Luke's gospel gave us the greatest commandment—that we are to love the Lord our God with all our heart, being, strength and mind and that we are to love our neighbor with mercy and compassion…even those that are different than us: the foundation of our call in how to treat others. And—skipping this week for a moment—next week Jesus teaches his disciples how to pray to the Father, giving us the prayer that we still recite to this day. So, as you can see, during these weeks of July we are given the basic tools of discipleship— we are called forth, we are given the foundational commandments and we are taught how to pray to our God. So, with all this, how does today's story of Martha and Mary fit in?

For we find Jesus entering a village and being welcomed by Martha while her sister Mary takes a disciple's position at the feet of Jesus. Seeing this is 1st century Jerusalem, a time where the Torah was never taught to women, it is important to note that in three instances Jesus is acting contrary to Jewish cultural norms. We find Jesus is alone with Jewish women who are not his relatives; a Jewish woman serves him food and lastly Jesus is teaching a woman in her own home. So by his behavior there is a clear underlying message that Jesus is giving everyone. The status quo is no longer. There is no separation of men and woman. The Word of God is for all. In short, by Jesus telling Martha that Mary has chosen a better way, he has in essence broken with Jewish law. And by allowing Mary to be sitting at his feet, he makes it very clear that all are called to hear his words. All are called to his table. All are called to his teachings. All of which is key to our call to discipleship.

It is this theme of table ministry and hospitality that Luke weaves throughout his Gospel. Versus Mark and Matthew, Luke has inserted 28 times the mention of house and home in his gospel. And this is why I feel we are given this story of Martha and Mary embedded in this tenth chapter which is focused on discipleship. The pure definition of hospitality is the cordial and generous relationship between guest and host. Henri Nouwen wrote that hospitality offers us the opportunity to deepen and broaden our insight into our relationship to our fellow human beings. And thus it is the core of discipleship. That is, if we are to be disciples and minister to each other, we must be in relationship not only with those we come across each day, but also with our God.

And if we are to fulfill our baptismal promises and be disciples of Christ, today's first reading and the Gospel calls for all of us to extend our tables within our families and to those around us. As a parish, there are a number of ways we do this, including our outreach to our sister parish in Africa, community programs we hold in the church, and serving others at table at our Cathedral in Trenton.

At home, you may have your own ways of how you spread your table to others that come into your life. For, like the meal Martha was preparing or that Abraham and Sarah prepared, physical nourishment is most often the way we extend our tables and our love to others.

Which reminds me of a story I once read, a table story that I thought would reflect the type of discipleship Christ calls us to. Actually the story comes from a cookbook called *Extending the Table*, written by Joetta Schlabach. For Joetta recognizes that many world cultures hold the preparation of food and the extension of their table to others as something core to their faith in God and love for others. And so the cookbook actually not only contains recipes from around the world, but is filled with insight and stories of the cultures behind the recipes and thus it is a book that nourishes the soul as much as it nourishes the body.

So the true story goes like this....

> Lesotho is a small, rural village in South Africa. Brenda was going to visit her friend Me Malebohang. Arriving at her house, Brenda found her at table in the courtyard, carving up a pumpkin. It was early winter, pumpkin harvesting time. Since pumpkins keep well, they are the main vegetable the Basotho, the people of Lesotho, eat during the winter.
>
> "What a bad harvest!" Me Malebohang said after they exchanged greetings. "More than half of the pumpkins rotted in my field. These eight are the only ones I have to keep for the winter."
>
> Time passed as their conversation flowed from talk of pumpkins to other topics. When Brenda rose to leave, Me Malebohang reached for one of her pumpkins on the wall and handed it to Brenda," Brenda protested. "You just told me that these are all you have for the winter!"
>
> Me Malebohang laughed. "We Basotho know that this is the way to do it. Next year I may have nothing in my field, and if I don't share with you now, who will share with me then?" Still smiling she took the pumpkin back from Brenda and cut it in half. "Here," she said, "you take this half and give the other half to your neighbor."
>
> "No matter how much food you have or how many guests you have, food will go around...when you share it, it goes around—it always does." *

No doubt the Basotho have learned and actively practice the message Christ gives us in today's Gospel. For you see, this gospel of Martha and Mary is not one that was written necessarily to show that a contemplative life is superior to one that is filled with action, or that Jesus necessarily prefers prayer over the preparation of a meal. Rather this gospel tells us of the radical steps Jesus took to bring his teachings to the home of Martha and Mary. Thus it reminds us that as baptized Christians we are all called to discipleship, we are all invited to partake of God's radical hospitality, and we are all sent to transform relationships so that they reflect the love of the risen Lord.

GEN. 18:20-32
COL. 2:12-14
LUKE 11:1-13

"So I tell you, ask and you will receive. Seek and you will find. Knock and the door will be opened."

Across the several readings today we actually have a rather comprehensive theology of prayer. From Genesis we heard the wonderful bargaining between Abraham and Yahweh. It gives one the impression that God can be bargained with – meaning that there is give and take. In any relationship there is the freedom to allow the other person to change us, to influence us. And this reading seems to say that even God allows our thoughts, our desires, our needs to matter to God.

And of course we hear Abraham whittle God down to ten just men. First, this becomes the basis for the notion of the ten just men, or the minion, the critical mass. That God is willing to deal with the whole because of a few; that all we need is a few to get it right. Later God calls it yeast, that all he needs is some yeast. So we see that God is saving history, the collective culture, all of us together. And somehow we're all caught up in this great sweep of God's love. Some lag behind. Some don't respond at all.

But thank God there are always at least ten just women, or ten just men, and we sort of ride on their coattails. All it takes is a few enlightened people in a parish or a neighborhood or a city, and it keeps the whole thing from going down the tubes. It is somewhat consoling to know that your little life might matter that much. And that you can actually somehow influence God. That God is not beyond caring. Isn't that good to know? That

God is not some kind of immovable mover up in the heavens and goes ahead with God's plan no matter what we say or do.

This becomes all unpacked in Luke's gospel where we hear his version of the Our Father which is a bit shorter than the one we are used to. In Matthew's version, the one we usually use, it's very clear that the prayer is also said as a collective. It's 'our Father', not just 'Father.' With that we address God together, not alone; not as a solitude. And that God is giving all of us, together, daily bread and forgiving our sins. With this we hear actually the only requirement for having your sins forgiven. And I suppose this is a little disappointing to Catholic priests who are used to thinking they alone can forgive sins. But, in fact, the prerequisite for having your sins forgiven is, do you forgive other people? That catches all of us. Do you forgive other people? If you do, then you will be forgiven. If you do not forgive other people, you will not be forgiven. You can only receive what you yourself give.

You would think in Christian history and Christian countries this concept would have created a much more forgiving people. But instead, every so often, we ran off to priests and went to confession instead turning to this universal forgiveness that we owe to all of those who we are holding debts against.

I was once teaching in South Africa and had occasion to spend time with Archbishop Desmond Tutu. One evening he was talking about his work in the healing of the races in South Africa. He said it required the free-dom to give up our right to our grievance. You see when you have even a legitimate grievance it becomes a right. It becomes something you think you deserve. You deserve to have one-upmanship over somebody else, and they deserve to be corrected or even punished.

Jesus seems to be saying in his great prayer that you have to give up the rights to your grievances because that is just a search for power; a search for superiority; a search to say, and a need to say to other people "gotcha". I gotcha. You did wrong and you owe it to me. This is not the soul speaking. This is not God speaking. This is what we call the ego—your need to feel wonderful about yourself and terrible about others.

Jesus makes, in his commentary on prayer, some rather absolute promises. He says if you ask you *will* receive. If you seek you *will* find. It's all about the asking. It's all about the seeking. I know this is going to strike you as unfair, but it isn't about getting what you want. It's about establishing the relationship; the relationship of trust. And if the relationship of trust is there, then he says don't worry; it's going to work out in the big picture.

And that's revealed in the very final wonderful line which doesn't seem to follow at all. Here you are asking for an egg or a fish, something practical that would feed your hunger, and he says if you, wicked as you are, know how to give good gifts to your children and if you, with your little ability to love, know how to give good gifts to your children, how much more will the heavenly Father give the Holy Spirit to those who ask him. Look, it doesn't even talk about us asking for the Holy Spirit. We were wanting an egg or a fish. He's not saying you're always gonna get what you want, but if you establish this life of communion and trust between yourself and the divine, you will be a recipient of the Holy Spirit. You will be a conduit of grace and freedom and healing for the world, and in the end, that's all that really matters. Then we'll probably forget about our momentary daily bread, our fish, or our egg. What we all want and what we all forever need…is the Holy Spirit.

18TH SUNDAY IN ORDINARY TIME

RICHARD G. MALLOY, S.J.

ECCLES. 1:2; 2:21-23
COL. 3:1-5, 9-11
LUKE 12:13-21

"One's life does not consist of possessions."

There was this guy who had a lot of riches. Loads of money. Tons of stocks and bonds. Big, big bucks. He gets a real slick lawyer and brings a lawsuit against heaven. He wants to bring his riches with him.

Now, heaven is a place where there are no lawsuits, but St. Peter figures he'll humor the guy and allow him to bring one suitcase with him. The guy dies. He shows up with a "suitcase" on wheels: eight feet long and six feet wide and five feet deep.

St. Peter says, "That's not a suitcase."

The guy says, "You didn't say anything about size."

St. Peter rolls his eyes and says, "Well I still have to open it and see what's in it."

The guy says, "Go ahead."

St. Peter opens the trunk and looks incredulously at hundreds and hundreds of bars of gold. He stares incredulously at the man and says, "You die, and you can bring a suitcase full of whatever riches you want to heaven, and you choose to bring pavement?"

Vanity of vanities profits us nothing. Vanity adds up to zilch, zip, nada.

St. Paul tells us to let go of the old man, or woman, and become our deepest truest selves in Christ. Let's set our hearts on things that matter and not on things that are just, well, things. The question to ask ourselves today is this: do we own our stuff or does our stuff own us? As daughters and sons of a loving God, we should recognize all we have is gift. We should use things in so far as they help us live happy and healthy and holy and free; we should divest ourselves of those things which entwine and ensnare our hearts.

Bishop Joseph Bambera of Scranton gave a wonderful homily to high school kids at Scranton Prep. He told them, "Someday everything I own will be owned by someone else." What a lot of elders in our society are finding is that their kids don't even want their "treasures." All this stuff accumulated over the years: the antique chair, the painting that adorned the living room wall, the 1989 big television. The kids don't want it. They're choking on all the crap they've accumulated. When you die what will happen to your possessions?

A few have so much, and so many have so little. 22% of America's children live in poverty. 15.1% of Americans are poor. That's 46.2 million people below the poverty line of $22,314 for a family of four. Globally, 80% of the people on planet earth live on less than $10 a day. Across our planet, 21,000 children die each day from preventable causes.

Meanwhile, CEOs of major U.S. corporations make 344 times what the average worker takes home. In 1980 they only earned 42 times a worker's pay. In 2004–2006, the average CEO in the U.S. made $13.3 million annually. Schoolteachers average $43,000 a year; David Letterman takes $31 million. Chief Justice John Roberts gets $217,000; Judge Judy walks away with $25 million. Median family income in the USA in 2010 was $49,445. Things are way out of whack.

The 400 wealthiest Americans have a greater combined net worth than the bottom 150 million Americans. The top 1 percent of Americans possesses more wealth than the entire bottom 90 percent. In the Bush expansion from 2002 to 2007, 65 percent of economic gains went to the richest 1 percent. What will the rich do with all they have? They can't take it with them. Why not share it now?

Br. Dennis Jude Ryan, S.J., spent most of his life as a Jesuit with the Oglala Sioux on the Pine Ridge reservation in South Dakota, the site of the infamous 1890 massacre at Wounded Knee. Br. Dennis died of a massive heart attack at the age of 35. His family and the Jesuits held a traditional Indian "give away" in his honor. Among the Lakota peoples, when someone dies, all their possessions are given away. Those who give away the most gifts to the members of the community are most respected. Such a cultural practice ensures that we have things, while not allowing things to own us.

Ponder the question put to the rich fool in today's Gospel: "To whom will all this piled up wealth of yours go?" Did the rich man think his riches impressed anyone? Did he think anybody really cared he was rich?

There's an old thought experiment. Name last year's MVP of the Super Bowl. Who won the Oscar this year for best actor? Who is the richest person in the world? Who is number two? Who was on the cover of People Magazine most often last year? Who won Celebrity Apprentice or Survivor last season? Does anyone in America "Got Talent"?

Now, name your first grade teacher. Name the best coach you ever had. Name the person who helped you get ahead in your occupation. Name your favorite Aunt or Uncle. Name the persons who love you. Name those you love.

You see? It's not our riches or accomplishments that impress. Those things barely matter. What really matters is who we love and who loves us. We are made to love and care for and cherish one another. Fame and fortune come and go with little rhyme or reason (how else explain

Snooki and "The Situation"?). Love and compassion, service and justice, faith and freedom: these, and the people and institutions that make them possible for us, last and endure. They last and make a lasting impression upon us.

Greed is not Good. Gordon Gekko in the movie Wall Street was wrong. Generosity trumps greed every time, no matter what Donald Trump says. Jesus tells us, "avoid greed in all its forms." Probably because he knows the greedy won't be at the heavenly banquet table.

There's an old image of heaven and hell. Hell is a place where there's this table laden with all kinds of succulent foods, wines, desserts. Thick juicy steaks, fat lobsters, crisp cool vegetables, every kind of pasta, delicious potatoes (hey, I'm Irish). Chocolate cakes. Ice cream. Pizza. Thin Mint Girl Scout cookies. And everyone in hell is sitting at the table emaciated and starving. Their arms don't bend at the elbows, so they cannot pick up the food and feed themselves. They spend eternity smelling the flavors and staring at the piles of food as their hungry, starving stomachs rumble. Heaven is exactly the same. All kinds of food, just like in hell. And in heaven everyone lacks elbows too. They cannot pick up food and feed themselves. But in heaven, everyone is fat and rosy cheeked and happy (with no high cholesterol or high blood pressure). How? Everyone in heaven, with those stiff arms, picks up the delicious food, and feeds the persons near them.

The opposite of poverty is not riches. The opposite of poverty is community. At this table of the Lord we are and become a community. Let us feast together. And let us pray.

WISD. 18:6-9
HEB. 11:1-2, 8-19
LUKE 12:32-48

"*Much will be required of the person entrusted with much*"

You can collect almost anything these days. The Franklin Mint is making a mint selling everything from replicas of antique cars to porcelain scenes from *Gone With the Wind*. When I was growing up, the mother of my best friend collected little Hummel figurines.

Well, I have a collection of my own: these three-dollar umbrellas. I must have 20 of them at home. I have one with the Velcro closure. I have one with the snap closure. I have one with a gold button. I have some with wooden handles. I have black ones and navy ones and tan ones. It all depends on where I was when the thunderstorm hit. And every time it happens, I tell myself, I'm not going to buy another one, and then about half a block from the subway, when I'm soaking wet, I give in and buy one at the newsstand. And then, a week or two later, when the weatherman is predicting rain, I forget it and go out of the house without one.

So what I'm about to say falls under the category of "Do as I say, not as I do."

Because I do exactly what Jesus tells us NOT to do in today's gospel. I end up not being prepared. And I get soaked. I sometimes think I'm single-handedly keeping the umbrella industry afloat.

But Christ today tells us something every Boy Scout knows by heart.

Be prepared.

Be like the servant who is awaiting the master's return. Have the lamps lit. Be at the door, ready to greet him.

There is an almost anxious tone to this gospel—and I suspect we often think of it in terms of the second coming, or the last judgment. Be prepared for Christ's return, and to have to give an accounting of your life. Be prepared to be judged.

That is part of it.

But I'd like to suggest another way of approaching this passage. Because this particular gospel is not about an ending...but a beginning.

Be prepared...for something wonderful.

Be prepared for God to come into your life.

Be prepared to open the door to Christ...and let him in, and to serve him.

In a way, this gospel is nothing less than a profound parable about vocations. Not just vocations as we know them, to religious life. But also, I think, the vocation to the Christian life.

Because we are all called. Each of us has a vocation, a calling to fulfill for God. But are we able to answer it? Are we listening for it?

Are we ready for whatever God wants us to do with our lives?

Are we looking for Him, anticipating Him?

Are we ready to give Him what He wants and needs—our time, our talent, even, perhaps, our lives?

Are we prepared?

Several years ago, I wrote and produced a documentary for the History Channel on the Kennedy family. And this gospel reading was one that Rose Kennedy drilled into her children again and again: "Much will be required of the person entrusted with much…and still more will be demanded of the person entrusted with more."

Her message to her children was this: because you are so well-off, because you have had advantages that others have not, you need to give something back. It undoubtedly had an impact. To this day, many of the Kennedys are committed to some form of public service, whether it's through politics, or the Special Olympics, or various forms of public advocacy.

But I think it's misguided to think of this as just referring to material wealth. After all, last week, we heard Christ telling his disciples that life does not consist of possessions.

No, I think this passage goes deeper. What we have been entrusted with can't be measured in dollars, or kept in a bank. People like the Kennedys won't be stashing it away in a safe deposit box or a trust fund.

We have been entrusted with something better, the most monumental gift: our faith. As the letter to the Hebrews puts it so eloquently, that faith "is the realization of what is hoped for, and evidence of things not seen." It is something beautiful and mysterious. And it is ours.

Our Catholic Christian faith has withstood two millennia of persecution and denial and doubt. And it has been passed on to us—the deposit of faith.

In short: we have been entrusted with much. And much will be required.

You can never know when God might come to your door, asking you to give something back.

Be prepared.

Be prepared…to love

Be prepared to feed the hungry...to shelter the homeless.

Be prepared to listen to a child who is hurting...or comfort a friend who is lonely...or pray for a stranger in intensive care.

Be prepared to stand up for those who have no one to stand up for them. The weak, the frightened, the old, the unborn.

Be prepared to live your life as a follower of Christ—a Christian. Because this faith is what we are, and what we have been given.

Much will be required of the person entrusted with much. And still more will be demanded of the person entrusted with more.

Look around you at the faith that has been handed to us. And look before you, to the tabernacle, where the Eucharist, Christ himself, waits for us. And look to the altar, where the greatest mystery of our faith is about to unfold.

We have been entrusted with everything.

What will we do with that?

This morning, we pray to be ready whenever God comes, for whatever He may ask us to do.

Light the lamp. Wait by the door. Be prepared.

Be prepared...for something wonderful.

And of course, if you don't remember anything else I've told you this morning, please remember this:

Don't leave home without your umbrella.

JER. 38:4-6, 8-10
HEB. 12:1-4
LUKE 12:49-53

"I have come to set the Earth on fire."

*I*t's *August but think Christmas.* Think of the angelic choir singing to the shepherds, "Glory to God in the highest and peace on earth…" Think of Handel's Messiah and think of its majestic words, "King of Kings!" and later, "Lord of Lords!" Then quickly fast forward to today's gospel with Jesus' words, "Do you think I have come to establish peace on the earth? No, I tell you, but rather division, so that even families will be divided among themselves." Strange words from the Prince of Peace! Until you remember that in John's gospel, on the night before he died, Jesus said, "I will ask the Father and he will give you another Advocate to be with you forever. Yes, this Spirit of truth whom, alas, the world cannot receive…."

That's the key, the word "truth." Prince of Peace that he is, Jesus would nevertheless speak truth, for peace cannot be built on a lie, and his Spirit would remind us of truth—but that, as Jesus noted, would be precisely the problem. The world cannot receive it and so would be divided. As the old Turkish proverb puts it, "Whoever says the truth will be chased out of nine villages." The world, it seems, cannot stand too much truth and the one who speaks it will often be tossed into the cistern, as was Jeremiah in today's first reading or, like Jesus, sent off to Calvary.

The fact is, the title "Prince of Peace" never implied that Jesus was harmless. The fact is truth-telling peace would always come at a price, because it would mean we would have to give up our habitual participation in the conspiracy of silences we maintain, silences we justify by saying, "Well, we want to keep the peace. We don't want to cause division. We don't want to rock the boat." But, for example, somewhere along the line the family has to stop pretending that Mom's drinking is not really a problem, the community has to stop pretending that it doesn't harbor racism, and the nation has to stop pretending that its economy is not based on the oppression of certain groups.

Sometimes the searing spotlight of truth is forced upon us like the recent, unspeakable horror of the abuse and killing of a mother and her two daughters in Connecticut. We see now that the criminal justice system failed, and failed miserably, to treat the two monstrous perpetrators as serious offenders, despite long, long histories of continuous, multiple crimes, repeatedly setting them free each time on parole. Like the devastating collapse of the Minneapolis bridge that has thrown the spotlight on lawmakers' shameless multi-billion dollar earmarks for pet political, vote-getting projects at the expense of the more unglamorous but basic maintenance of roads and transit projects badly in need of repair and upgrading.

The divisions truth causes go on. As I speak to you, Christians in the Sudan, China, and Saudi Arabia are literally dying for their faith. That's perhaps hard for us to understand, we who, in the name of tolerance, are afraid of alienating anyone, but the fact is, there will always be a sense of exclusion for anyone who holds a truth. Orthodox Jews don't want to be forced to give up their dietary laws. Quakers don't want to be forced to serve in the military. Fundamentalist Christians don't want evolution taught to their children. We don't have to agree with them, only to acknowledge the fact that openly adhering to a belief system is what religion is all about and it does cause division. Yet we know that if we dare to speak truth we may earn the dreaded label of intolerant.

But we must remember that "intolerance" means disagreement with punishment, as pogroms, inquisitions, and forced sensitivity training sessions testify. True tolerance, on the other hand, is disagreement but without punishment. But it's still disagreement and we are right, without rancor and with charity, to make challenges and to bear witness. We can't do this, we can't set the world on fire, if we have politically corrected tolerance to mean "live and let live."

A false tolerance means no judgment, no witness, no truth, no divisions. False tolerance says, "You must approve of what I do." The Christian response is, "I must do something harder: I will love you even when your bad behavior—and it is that—offends me." False tolerance says, "You must agree with me." The Christian response is, "I must do something harder: I will tell you the truth because I'm convinced the truth will set you free." False tolerance says, "You must allow me to have my way." The Christian response is, "I must do something harder. I will plead with you to follow the right way because I believe you are worth the risk." False tolerance, in a word, seeks to be inoffensive; Christian tolerance takes risks. False tolerance costs nothing; Christian tolerance costs everything.

In our misguided and intimidated commitment to false tolerance we duck even the minor divisions. Unlike that famous *Saturday Evening Post* magazine cover by Norman Rockwell, we are afraid to bless ourselves and say grace at Wendy's or McDonald's, much less at an upscale restaurant lest we offend somebody. When we're greeted with the politically correct "happy holidays," we hesitate to respond with a pleasant "Merry Christmas." We send our secular friends secular Christmas cards so we won't upset them, rather than bless them from our tradition.

Some of our bedrooms are devoid of crucifixes and our homes frequently religiously sanitized so that no one who doesn't know us suspects we're Catholic. Our magazine racks contain everything from O to *Vogue*, *Newsweek* to *Newsday*, but nothing to hint that we are committed to a different way of life. We sometimes, even passively, participate in the worst kind of smutty conversation because walking away or protesting would make us appear intolerant or earn us unsavory labels. We're not always much good in establishing division, the line between vice and virtue, good and evil, right and wrong. We're no Rosa Parks in December 1955 who divided a nation when she offensively clung to her seat when ordered by the bus driver, J.P. Blake, to the back of the bus.

"He offended no one" is, when you think about it, a rather accusatory motto on a gravestone. And far, far from the true peace that brings division.

The fact is, we are known as much as for our silences as for our actions, for our efforts at peace as well as for the truth that divides and challenges. As another old proverb goes, "The candle says to the darkness, 'I beg to differ.'" Our Christian lives should be a candle—"Let your light shine in the darkness," Jesus said—and if the darkness is offended, so be it. Setting the earth on fire is a skill Christians have to acquire.

Taken from Once Upon a Gospel: Inspiring Homilies and Insightful Reflections *by William J. Bausch (New London, CT: Twenty-Third Publications), 2008.*

ISA. 66:18-21
HEB. 12:5-7, 11-13
LUKE 13:22-30

"Some are last who will be first, and some are first who will be last"

When I was reminiscing with a friend's father, he told me, "Things were so different when I was your age. You know, there used to be a time when you would have a dinner party with Democrats and Republicans. Nobody thought a thing about it!"

I was outraged. At first I thought, *We have dinner parties with Democrats and Republicans!* But then I remembered that the only time that we had a social event with mixed company was with my family of origin. And even that was somewhat strained whenever the conversation began to drift over to the latest MSNBC or Fox News headlines.

I was a pastor in Washington, D.C. for seven years. After being there for a while, things begin to look a bit differently. So many people worked in politics that we began to walk around like we were wearing old-fashioned 3-D glasses, with one red lens and one blue lens. When people met me, they assumed that I was one or the other.

Many of my friends thought in terms of red and blue maps. They had the geography of the entire country memorized so that if you mention a state, or even a large city, they could recite the political views of the average citizen. They were good at their jobs, they had done their homework, they had read the polls, and they had determined who we are.

Sometimes when I read the newspaper, this sort of lack of imagination spills out on the page. It seems as if the media would love to paint us into red or blue corners. Then they could just hand out a set of talking points to tell us what we believe. It would make life easier. We no longer have to sit down with our neighbors and listen to their complicated views. We don't have to hear their messy individual stories untangling. We know who they are. Depending on age, gender, education, ethnicity, geography, and whether we are a tomato or a blueberry, we can know a person's views on religion, how much money they make, and—for the most part—what they think. It's a very efficient way of determine who's on and who's off of the dinner party list.

Other times, especially when the tactic is being used on me, I feel like a tiny pawn in a giant chess game. Someone has made up rules, deciding that I ought to accept certain things as true and if I do not believe them completely, then I am on the wrong side of the chessboard. Throughout all of it, we manipulate people. We encourage people to think as a herd and we use social shunning to assimilate them into political parties. Then people look at my Facebook page or find out what I believe on one or two issues to determine whether I am part of "us" or "them."

For all of our hope for unity and love, as Christians the polarities can be worse. In my particular denomination, the Presbyterian Church (USA), we can see how we are breaking into factions over political issues as much as theological ones.

Perhaps it wasn't much different from Jesus' time. The issues have varied a bit, but we can still hear the "who's out and who's in" conversation among the followers of Jesus. Someone asks Jesus, "Lord, will only a few be saved?" From the context, it sounds like the person wants to be able to have those tidy labels—whether they are based on a person's ethnicity, gender, or beliefs.

Jesus doesn't seem to have much patience with the question. If I may paraphrase, it's as if Jesus is saying, "Just aim for the narrow gate. Assume that you're all outsiders and try the best that you can. Don't try to assess who is in and who is out. Don't even waste your time on all of that because you're not going to be able to figure it out. The last will be first and the first will be last."

What if we *really* led our lives in this manner? What if we met each person and had no preconceived notions about who they were, but listened to their stories and understood their human messiness? What if we set aside our various litmus tests to determine to which camp a person ought to belong? What if we did not scroll a person's Facebook page to see what sort of interests they had in order to put some defining label upon them? What if we just assumed that they were outsiders like we were outsiders and we took the time to get to know the mystery of another human being? What if we did not try to manipulate and control the outcomes of our human relationships?

As Christians, what if we didn't assume that we were always the one of the few fitting in that gate? What if we had a bit of humility and assumed the position of outcasts who are just trying the best that we can? What if we understood that we were all in the same place, and striving to do our best in the midst of it?

I daresay, if we set aside all of the ways in which we determine who is in and who is out, if we begin to relate to one another as mysteries, as outsiders who (like ourselves) are trying to fit in but just can't quite do it, we would have a very different sort of faith.

SIR. 3:17-18, 20, 28-29
HEB. 12:18-19, 22-24A
LUKE 14:1, 7-14

"When you hold a banquet invite the poor."

"On a Sabbath Jesus went to dine at the home of one of the leading Pharisees, and the people there were observing him carefully."

In Luke's original Greek, "observing him carefully" has the same meaning as Obama observing Hillary Clinton carefully or Giuliani observing Romney carefully. They were not observing to pick up pointers. They were watching carefully for their opponents to trip themselves up: some politically incorrect slip of the tongue, some gaffe, some slight contradiction. And then they would pounce. That's the "watching carefully" of the gospel. The irony, of course, was that, at the same time, Jesus was watching them carefully.

What he saw was the usual social climbing and jockeying for position. That's normal human pride at work and it's something to be dealt with, and so, on this level, Jesus offers some practical wisdom which adds up to, "Don't embarrass yourself. Don't sit at the head table only to be publicly escorted to the main dining room when the guest of honor arrives. Don't be like the latecomer at a wedding who sits in the empty seat in the front pew, the one reserved for the bride's mother. Don't rush into the taxi waiting to pick up a celebrity. And don't park in Father's spot!"

That's everyday etiquette advice to soften up his audience. Then Jesus hits them with the real point: Don't always invite your in-group against whom you are always measuring yourself, but measure yourself against the less fortunate; that is, let your heart, your charity, and your compassion move beyond the people who can pay you back. Jesus says in effect, "Be like your heavenly Father who sends rain on the just and unjust alike and invite the least of your brethren, those who have no voice, those who never receive an invitation and from whom nothing can be expected.

A strong gospel point, so let me give you an example of how it's done. I'll tell you about a man who heroically extended a lifelong invitation to those with absolutely nothing to offer. His name is Peter Claver, a seventeenth-century Spaniard, whose feast is on September 9. His invitees were slaves.

For over a thousand years, slavery, long an institution, had died out over time, slavery in Europe at least. By the twelfth century it was virtually unknown. But then, dramatically, in the fifteenth century, European exploration and exploitation of Africa, Asia, and the Americas revived the slave trade with a vengeance. The Portuguese explorers who followed the coast of Africa in search of new trade routes to Asia saw money-making opportunities everywhere they went. With their superior weapons, it was easy to conquer the local people, and it was a short step from subduing a population to enslaving them.

As one of the first new lands colonized by the Portuguese, the Canary Islands became the first place where slavery was reintroduced. But when word of the situation reached Pope Eugenius IV in 1435, he fired off a letter to the local bishop denouncing the enslavement of the Canary Islanders and demanding that they be set free. His plea fell on deaf ears as the Portuguese and then the Spanish pushed farther and farther into fabulously wealthy unknown lands and the temptation to exploit the riches of these territories through the slave labor of the local population became irresistible. Besides, the explorers argued, those American Indians, Africans, and Asians were clearly less than human, quite inferior, brutish, primitive beings. Pope Paul III fired back with a 1537 document that asserted that "the Indians themselves indeed are true men" and that "no one in any way may presume to reduce said Indians to slavery."

Forget the pope. In spite of papal condemnations, greed won out and the international slave trade flourished among Catholics and Protestants for another four hundred years and often, by the way, with the cooperation of the native blacks who grew rich by rounding up and selling their fellow citizens.

In the midst of all this, a son, Peter, was born to the Clavers, a farming family who worked the land in the province of Catalonia in Spain. He was a bright, religious lad, but like Hamlet, he found it very hard ever to make a decision and stick with it. His parents eventually sent Peter to a school run by the Jesuits in Barcelona. At that time the Jesuits were still a relatively new religious order in the Catholic Church. They soon became not only renowned teachers and shock troops against the Protestant Reformation, but famous as missionaries and convert makers as well.

Such an active, exciting, varied life appealed to Peter. He talked a lot about joining but could never quite commit himself. Finally, after vacillating for several years, Peter Claver asked to be received as a Jesuit novice. But, typical Peter, he had barely entered the novitiate when he began once more to second-guess himself. What if he was not cut out for an active life as a missionary or parish priest? Maybe this, maybe that. He drove everyone crazy.

Fortunately, help was nearby in the person of the college doorkeeper, a seventy-two-year-old lay brother named Alphonsus Rodriguez. Brother Alphonsus had had a family and a career, but after his wife and children all died, he gave up his business and entered the religious life. Although he was a Jesuit brother now, he hadn't lost his ability, cultivated over many years as a businessman, to judge character. Nor had he lost his knack for handling a customer who couldn't decide what he wanted. So it was Brother Alphonsus who assured Peter that he did indeed belong with the Jesuits and, moreover, that Peter should ask his superiors to send him to the Americas as a missionary. Peter was stunned. But Brother Alphonsus insisted that the way to overcome fear and indecision is make a bold move.

So Peter summoned up his courage and asked his superiors to assign him to the American mission. They gave their consent and sent him to Cartagena, Colombia, as an unordained novice.

Now Cartagena's location on the Caribbean Sea made it one of the principal ports for the slave trade in the New World: twelve thousand enslaved Africans were unloaded in Cartagena every year. You can imagine that, after weeks crammed together in the dark holds of the slave ships, these tragic people were filthy, weak from hunger and dehydration, and half mad with fear. Many were sick. Some were dying. Yet, whatever their condition, all were driven like cattle into holding pens near the dock to be sorted out and sold later. The only white man who treated the Africans kindly was a Jesuit priest, Father Alphonsus de Sandoval. When he heard the roar of the harbor cannon that signaled the arrival of another slave ship, Father de Sandoval gathered up food, water, and medicine and hurried down to the harbor. The comforts Father de Sandoval could offer the Africans were meager, yet he cared for his "parishioners," as he called them, day after day until they had all been sold off and the pen was empty.

When Peter Claver, the apprehensive new Jesuit recruit from Spain, arrived in Cartagena, Father de Sandoval made him his assistant. At first glance it would appear that the priest had made a terrible mistake. Yet this turned out to be the turning point for Peter. The work in the slave pen transformed him, this well-off, middle-class young man. Once he recognized that he could do something for God and his fellow man, all doubts, all qualms, all uncertainties vanished. He asked his superiors in Cartagena to ordain him and to permit him to serve the slaves. A saint-in-the-making had been born. He would spend the rest his life inviting to the Lord's banquet the poor, the crippled, the blind—those who could never repay.

Every time a slaver sailed into Cartagena's harbor, Peter took the pilot's boat out to the ship and began his work at once down in the hold. On shore, as sailors and soldiers herded the slaves into the pens, Peter went with them. Over the years he built up a team of interpreters who could speak the languages of Guinea, the Congo, and Angola, the lands from which most of the captives came. Through his interpreters Peter tried to comfort the Africans and learn what they needed. Every day Peter and his interpreters returned with more food, more water, more medicines, and as he treated the Africans, he explained to them the basics of the Catholic faith. It is said that during the forty-four years Father Claver served in the slave pens, he baptized over one hundred thousand Africans. Whatever the number of converts may have been, Peter regarded them as his parishioners. He kept up a steady round of visitations, saying Mass for his converts, bringing them the sacraments, and continuing their religious instruction.

No surprise, Peter Claver's devotion to his African converts enraged the white population of Cartagena. The charges: He was keeping slaves from their work. He was contaminating churches and chapels with his congregations of unwashed Africans. He was profaning the Blessed Sacrament by giving Communion to these "animals." Some well-born ladies even refused to enter a church if Father Claver had said Mass there for slaves. Even some of Peter's brother Jesuits thought he was excessively devoted to the Africans. No matter. After years of wavering, Peter Claver had found his vocation, and he would not be deterred from it.

Peter kept up his exhausting routine until one day, when he was seventy-four years old, he collapsed in the slave pen. Back at the Jesuit residence he lay on his deathbed, abandoned by the white Christians of Cartagena. The only one who tried to nurse the dying man was an African servant. The end came quickly. Late in the evening on September 7, 1654, Peter Claver received the last sacraments, then fell unconscious and died shortly after midnight. A crowd of slaves broke down the gates of the Jesuit residence so they could see their saint one last time.

On January 15, 1888, the people of Rome witnessed a double canonization as Pope Leo XIII declared that Peter Claver and Alphonsus Rodriguez, banquet throwers for the poor, were saints.

And that, my parishioners, is this gospel of the Lord.

Taken from Once Upon a Gospel: Inspiring Homilies and Insightful Reflections *by William J. Bausch (New London, CT: Twenty-Third Publications), 2008.*

Wɪs. 9:13-18ʙ
Pʜɪʟᴇᴍ. 9ʙ-10, 12-17
Lᴜᴋᴇ 14:25-33

"Whoever does not carry his own cross and come after me cannot be my disciple."

I'd like to go on a diet.

A lot of you might say, quietly, "Well, it's about time, Father!" Even under these vestments, it's clear to everyone that a little less food, and a lot more exercise, is in order. And I agree! But I'm not talking about that kind of diet. You see, there's only one food I'm tempted to give up this morning. Jesus gives us a description of his "Discipleship Sandwich"—and I'm afraid it sounds a little tough to digest.

The two slices of bread in this sandwich are "Renounce Your Family" and "Renounce Your Possessions." And in between is the toughest meat imaginable: "Carry Your Cross." This Discipleship Sandwich must have been just as hard to digest when he described it to the crowds on his way to Jerusalem two thousand years ago, as it is today. Nobody I know would voluntarily order this sandwich. And I wouldn't be surprised if those who did order it only get a few bites into it before leaving it, unfinished, on the table.

Renounce your family. Carry your cross. Renounce your possessions.

There's got to be something wrong with that sandwich. There's too much cholesterol. Too many calories. Too many carbohydrates. And Jesus doesn't even offer a tasty drink to wash it all down.

It would be great if we could avoid this Discipleship Sandwich completely. But I'm here to tell you that, if we want to be Christians, or if we want to *remain* Christians, it's the only thing on the menu. Except, of course, for Christ's own renunciation and Cross—his Body and Blood—which we continue to eat and drink as "food for the journey."

There's a lot of priests and deacons having a tough time preaching this morning. Because today is called "Hard Gospel Sunday." There doesn't seem to be any way to get around the fact that Jesus was deadly serious. (After all, he was on his way to Jerusalem, and he knew what awaited him there.) He was clearly letting everyone know that being his disciple is going to *cost* us something. Just as it was going to cost *him* everything. It was "truth in advertising"—and he wasn't about to sugarcoat what "being a disciple" means.

I wish I could go on a diet and avoid this one sandwich. I don't want to renounce my family. I don't want to renounce my possessions. And I certainly don't want to carry my cross. But when I look up at the Menu Board, I've got to remember that I'm not at McDonald's. I'm not here to be "McSaved" and I don't want to be a "McChristian." I'm standing in line for *real* salvation. And the Lord is calling me to be a *real* Christian.

So I'm putting off that diet. And I'm ordering the Discipleship Sandwich. (And I want the Quarter Pounder, please!) I'm going to remember that "hating my family" and "renouncing my possessions" simply means not letting my relationships or my things get in the way of "looking for the cross," or "embracing the cross" when I find it. "Renouncing" is hard; but it's not impossible.

Now, when I *am* at McDonald's, especially at the drive-thru, the cashier usually throws in all kinds of things I might need: salt and pepper packets, a little tub of dipping sauce for my chicken tenders, ketchup for my fries, sugar for my coffee, a straw for my milkshake—and a fistful of napkins, too. You get a lot of free stuff at McDonald's! (Enough for your own little landfill.)

Well, with the Discipleship Sandwich, the Lord throws in some stuff, too. And it's all free. Look in the bag, and inside, there are packets of mercy and forgiveness. There are little tubs of love and compassion.

Salvation's in there, too. It's down at the bottom of the bag: Just look for it!

| Exod. 32:7-11, 13-14
1 Tim. 1:12-17
Luke 15:1-32 | *"Rejoice with me because I have found my lost sheep"* |

We live in a society that loves to accumulate stuff and loves to get rid of stuff. You can buy things to help you organize, or you can really go for simple living and cast things off. This has helped launch things like Freecycle a website that helps you give things away for free, rather than throw them out. It also helped spawn the freegans. They are dedicated to the idea that "one person's trash is another's treasure."

The freegan movement can be ideologically, economically, or ecologically motivated, but it is always pointed towards the recovery of what others have deemed worthless. Freegans believe that our society is wasteful—that our society throws away things that could be put to good use. Their guiding principle is to salvage what others have carelessly tossed away.

For some freegans, this means "dumpster diving" for food, clothing, or furniture. It could mean scouting out curbsides the evening before trash day. Freegans are in search of stuff to reuse and repurpose by giving new life to what would otherwise be rubbish.

Some freegans squat in vacant houses. Apparently, a few squatter settlements have become places for people on the margins. Those with no place to go can sleep, clean up, and eat in a freegan house. For these outcasts, a freegan squat is a place of welcome in a world that might ignore or revile them. For their freegan hosts, this is another way to turn the trash into a treasure—of the human sort.

This notion of turning trash into treasure is challenging. Would I go dumpster diving? At supermarkets, food is often packaged and non-perishable but bears expiration dates that render it unsellable. Is it unusable? With shame, I admit that a can of soup that expired last week pulled from the dumpster might seem unappetizing to me. However, the food is still good; it is usable and nourishing, so why not eat it? Isn't that good stewardship?

As we struggle to understand this, today's Gospel from Luke offers us a trio of parables that ask us, "What is trash and what is treasure?" And who decides who or what is trash or treasure? Before the parables begin we hear "the tax collectors and sinners were all drawing near to listen to him." Jesus is calling forth those at the edges, frequently upsetting those who are in power. Could this be a way of turning the trash of society into treasure?

It seems that way, doesn't it? Jesus is dedicated to the pursuit of what appears undesirable and unusable in the form of human persons. Tax collectors and sinners in first century Palestine were low on the social scale. Like a freegan host in a squatter's mansion, Jesus opens the door to give nourishment, refreshment, rest and hope to those who would enter.

What about a shepherd missing one sheep out of a hundred? Every sheep matters, as does each person. The shepherd must find and care for the sheep, which are both livelihood and gift from God. A coin is inanimate but still important. The woman who loses one is determined to reclaim what God has given to her. Each coin matters, as does each person. Each sheep, each coin, each person—they all have value, especially the person.

Perhaps that is why the last parable is the longest, and most powerful. In the story of the Prodigal Son, we hear of a man who had a son who left home.

This son does the unthinkable and asks for his inheritance while his father is still alive. While many fathers of that time would have disowned their son, this father gives the son his share. In an ultimate act of scandal, the son departs and lives riotously. The father waits and longs for his son's return. It seems that God is always willing to take a chance on us, too, even when we ask for things and then take off without a backward glance.

After squandering everything, the son ends up tending swine, the most unclean of creatures, not to be touched by a good Jew under any circumstances. In a freegan-like move, the starving son eats what the swine do not, consuming what he could dig up, in the worst part of the trash. There would have been no way for him to be considered worthy or pure after this, but he did what he had to do to in order to survive. He felt sorrow and regret and thought about returning home.

Going home was unimaginable, yet that is what the son does, expecting little or nothing in return. His father is waiting for him, which is another unbelievable element in this story. Shouldn't the father be furious? However, his father welcomes him joyfully and throws a big welcome home party as this son is embraced back into the fold. His son is not trash, but treasure!

Our first reading from the Book of Exodus reveals God's frustration with his people. "Stiff-necked" is what God called them in His anger. Yet Moses prevails, asking God for mercy and, amazingly, God "changed His mind." God will continue to care for His people with love.

The second reading, from the first letter to Timothy, reiterates the theme of salvaging the unsalvageable. Reconciling mercy and forgiveness are at the heart of Christ, who comes to redeem us. We hear of Saul, once a great blasphemer, who meets Christ, experiences conversion, and becomes Paul. Of course, Paul goes on to become the one who spreads the Gospel in the most profound way.

These messages remind us that we often view others or even view ourselves as potentially unusable, disposable and unredeemable. Yet Jesus is here to turn that on its head! In God's eyes, no one is disposable!

At a time when we routinely hear about who should be excluded from government, society, or church, the Word of God speaks to us clearly. God's mercy and forgiveness, God's reconciling power, trumps all. No human person is trash; each human person is a treasure. We are all called to see and offer that to each other.

So what are we to do? That may be the hardest part of all. How can we make sense of this in our own lives? Should I not throw stuff away? Or become a freegan?

For one person this might mean reconciling with a rejected relative. For another, it might mean forgiving a friend—no matter whose fault it was. It might mean choosing not to view someone with disdain if their politics are different from ours. It could mean that we choose not to be suspicious of the person sitting next to us in the pew simply because that person sees church differently than we do. Ultimately, this might mean that when we look in the mirror, we choose not to loathe the person who gazes back at us.

In the Kingdom of God, no person is beyond repair, no person is to be thrown away. In the Kingdom of God, every person is to be welcomed, cherished, loved and saved through Christ the Lord. In the Kingdom of God, there is no human trash—we are all treasure.

| Amos 8:4-7 |
| 1 Tim. 2:1-8 |
| Luke 16:1-13 |

"You cannot serve both God and mammon."

Today we celebrate the 25th Sunday in Ordinary Time, which has been designated by the American Catholic Bishops as Catechetical Sunday. For on the third Sunday of September, across the United States, we pause as a community to celebrate and applaud those who minister by teaching our faith. It is a time that we recognize and give thanks to those teachers and volunteers who work within our parish. It is a time to remind our catechists and all of us gathered here that we are called by God to use the talents that we have been given.And it is this last point that leads us to look at today's Gospel—one that is often labeled one of the most often misunderstood Gospels: the story of the Master and the Steward. For at first glance, it could seem that Jesus is actually supporting the concept of swindling your neighbor! But, like all of his parables, if you peel away the layers and drop this into first-century context, the message that Christ's parable brings to us today becomes clear.

You see, this is a story of a Steward who is entrusted with selling his Master's goods. His job is to take his master's inventory, apply a nominal mark-up for his pay and sell the goods to those around the area. Evidently, the Steward was very good at what he did, as he was able to place a significant mark-up or interest payment on top of the Master's costs and still make the sale. But the wise Master recognized that by the Steward gouging the customers with high interest rates that the market would not continue to pay for his goods. Thus the Steward was mismanaging the assets. So while short term, the Master was making his margin, although his customers were overpaying…long term, he knew his sales would fall. So he dismissed the Steward, not for being dishonest, but rather for not being prudent. Clearly by misusing his talents, the Steward was focused on short term gain versus long term growth.

So once the Steward realizes that the gravy train has ended and that he has lost his job, he sees that he has few options to make a living. And so now he becomes focused on his future—where he is going and how he will be accepted by others. He now realizes placing his trust and his talents into short term financial gain did not bring him true rewards. So using the same financial talents that got him into trouble in the first place, he does a life course correction, and rewrites the debtor's notes, removing his abnormally high interest mark-ups.

Through this act of reformation, it is these actions—this use of his talents that are commended by the Master and at the same time certainly welcomed by the debtors. He thereby positions himself to be praised by the Master and welcomed into the community.

So how can we apply this parable to our lives and our spiritual journey? The Lord has indeed entrusted each and every one of us with many talents and assets for us to manage. How are we using them? Are we simply focused on the here and now…what looks good…what feels good…what is popular…and the quickest way to make a buck? When we take inventory of our goods, our gifts and the abilities God gave us, do we take the time to ask ourselves how well we are managing and using our talents?

Bringing us back to this celebration of Catechetical Sunday—it is these same questions that Archbishop Dolan raises in his recent article on the state of Catholic education in the United States and its steady decline in numbers. Since 1960, the number of schools has gone from 13,000 to 7,000, and the number of students from 5.2 million to 2.1 million.

He goes on to list the number of reasons for the decline but indicates that the most crippling reason is the shift in American Catholic thinking. Namely that many have disavowed their school systems, excusing themselves from any further involvement with a Catholic school, simply because their children are not enrolled in the school or religious ed program. Dolan reminds us that, "Catholic education is a communal and ecclesial duty and not just for parents of school children." In short, for Catholic education to thrive, it requires the whole ecclesia, the whole church—i.e. all of its members, without exception, to use our gifts and their talents, coming together for a common cause. So, we at St. Paul's are very grateful to those who give of their talents to support our school and Religious Ed program.

But as we honor and bless our teachers, let us keep in mind that the reason Catholic education is so important is that our teachers do more than just teach the faith—they institute, nurture, and cultivate personal change in our children. The word 'catechize' means to teach by word of mouth *in order to promote a change or transformation in another*. So while we live in this highly visual world of video, internet, email, text messages, and books, catechism in the early church and still today requires this verbal storytelling and careful listening. It is one reason why we proclaim the readings in our liturgies: so that the words will be heard…so that the words will teach…so that the words will transform.

But it is not enough to only recognize our Religious Education teachers on this Catechetical Sunday. For the US Catholic Conference of Bishops selected the theme of this year's Catechetical Sunday to be "Matrimony: Sacrament of Enduring Love." It was Pope John Paul II who stated that building a "civilization of love" starts at the heart of the family—with the parents.

So this is also a time to remind all parents of our responsibility as primary teachers in the family—providing for our children's spiritual education. It is a promise we made in our wedding vows: that we will accept children lovingly from God and raise them well in the Catholic Faith. It is the call that is embedded in the final blessing that we received at the baptism of our children: we are to be the first and best teachers of our children. And it is a mission that does not end at our child's Confirmation, but rather lasts a lifetime by what we say and do.

But besides teachers and parents, on this Catechetical Sunday we also need to remember that *all* of us are called to catechize. When St. Paul was describing the gifts God had given the church, he listed teaching as one of the most important. And the last mandate of Jesus to all was to go and teach! So, too, just as the disciples at Pentecost were sent to teach, we are called to be a people of action—to bring forth Christ to others. By virtue of our baptism we are *all* sent forth to teach....it is not limited to only religious education teachers or to parents. All of us are charged to catechize, all of us are tasked with teaching others, all of us are called to use our talents that God has given us, and in doing so we transform ourselves, we transform our children, we transform each other.

And that is why we gather here each week at this Eucharistic celebration—to be nourished and to nourish others. It was the Jesuit theologian Robert Taft who said that the purpose of Eucharist is not to only change bread and wine, but to change you and me—for through Eucharist it is we who are to become Christ for others.

For, indeed, this Sunday calls us all to be teachers of God's word....to be Christ to others....for today's "good news" challenges us to be stewards of the gifts we have received, not sprinting for a short-term gain, but rather running a marathon, on the long road we call our spiritual journey to God's kingdom.

Amos 6:1ᴀ, 4-7 1Tɪᴍ. 6:11-16 Luke 16:19-31	*"Father Abraham, have pity on me"*

When we gather as a community, we witness the greatness of the Lord because we are his family and his people. And because we're his family, Christ tells us stories because he likes us to grow in the awareness of who we are.

In the reading of the Rich Man and Lazarus Jesus takes a common story that his own folks would have heard many times and he starkly contrasts two men. One is in purple garments and he wants us to realize that that person is very, very, very rich, probably of noble birth. He is one who not only dines well, he also holds the absolute desire to want to dine well: he wants to be that kind of a person. Jesus then tells us about poor Lazarus. He can't get enough food from the scraps and the Rich Man just passes him by.

When Jesus would tell this story, what many first heard was that the Rich Man was blessed by God, in as much that the more you got, the better of a person you must have been and that is why God gave you all of these nice things. And that the converse is true: that if you were a bad person you would have suffered on earth and all these things would have happened to you. But it is the difference that Jesus wants to make sure we understand. For in the end it was Lazarus who is carried to the bosom of Abraham by the angels and the Rich Man undergoes the torments of

Hades. What Jesus was telling His people, and tells us today, is that God's reign is in the everyday affairs of our lives, that God's kingdom is where we see it and feel it and hope for it. So, Jesus puts us on alert that even in the midst of our daily affairs we'll find the reign of God.

I guess if the Rich Man had the insight he certainly would have acted differently. The reign of God, Jesus was saying, came to that Rich Man disguised as an ulcerated homeless victim. The Rich Man missed his opportunity to share in the Reign of God. The awareness in the Reign of God is to see the Lazaruses in our daily life in a radically new context. So, Jesus gives us something to ponder and so I offer these questions to you: How does the reign of God enter your life? And how do you respond?

In response to the second question, think of the message that you would have Jesus say to his brothers and sisters. If Jesus asked me that question, I'd say, "Well, I know you're a good storyteller, Jesus, so I'd give you a story for you to tell, like this."

Emma was a very busy woman, very successful; she would fly all over and do her work. But, like many of us, she got tired and was just looking for a little space of time and a little place of solitude to be by herself. So, on the way to the airport she decided that once there, she would find a nice little chair and wait for her flight, be by herself and read a book. So once there, she checked in and found a quiet place. A few minutes later, an old woman came by and sat down next to her. After a few minutes the old woman said, "I bet it's cold in Chicago." And Emma said, "Yeah, I guess so." The old woman kept asking her questions and talking and all the while Emma answered her curtly and coldly. And finally, the old woman said, "I am going to Chicago, to bring my husband back. We were married 53 years and he died suddenly. I'm bringing his body back to Chicago." Emma put her book down and she reached out and she held the old woman's hand. And they talked and talked, and she realized that this old woman needed someone to listen to her—even if a stranger. Soon the call was made to board the plane and so they walked together. Emma was a few rows in back of the old lady, and as she was stuffing her coat up in the rack, saw the old lady take her seat. Soon a young man sat down next to her and Emma heard the old lady say to the young guy, "I bet you it's cold in Chicago." All Emma could do was say a little prayer that the young man would listen.

You know we are all rich, aren't we—and I am not talking about monetary wealth. We don't realize how rich we are. We have so much: the love of parent and child, the love for each other. We can be educated, we can study, we can eat, we can play games, we can root for our favorite team or whatever we do but we've got lots of good things. So take a step back and see how much you can do for God's Kingdom, for there is so much more to be done. So, I urge you to let that faith really grow inside of you. I urge you to study hard, play hard and have friendships that are strong and hard but always know at the center there is Christ.

Because on the other hand we're all Lazarus, aren't we? We're all kind of poor, we all need help, we all need to be healed, and we all make mistakes. And God somehow puts it all together. At each of our liturgies we offer peace to each other. I'm not even quite sure that all of us understand what that peace is really supposed to be. It's so easy to say, "Peace of the Lord be with you." "Shalom" is the greeting for the Jewish people when they come together. But "Shalom" is the greeting of the Jewish people as they leave. Where Jesus would say Shalom to his brother, he was really offering them be one with the harmony of all of creation. To be one with the musical chords of a band: the concert of life. To be one—that is what that peace is all about.

So the next time you offer that Shalom, I hope you realize that there are many, many ways to say, "I bet it's cold in Chicago." The next time someone comes up to us and says, "Hey, can you help me with my school work, can you help me with my papers, can you listen to my story." They are really saying, "I bet you it's cold in Chicago." If someone ever comes forward and says, "Yeah, I made a mistake, I'm pregnant, I am thinking of an abortion." Maybe they are really saying, "It's cold in Chicago." They need our help. Or maybe it's just somebody sitting on the curb for a meal and we tend to pass them by. Perhaps they are just saying, "You know what? I bet you it's cold in Chicago."

I hope you take time to meditate a bit on where the reign of God breaks into your daily lives and what to do about it. Because when we share with each other peace and Shalom, no doubt, we are in harmony with God; with his word, with his Eucharist. For God asks us to be his instruments, to sing a new song and to bring it to those who ask, Shalom.

You know, I bet you it's cold in Chicago.

HAB. 1:2-3, 2:2-4

2 TIM. 1:6-8, 13-14

LUKE 17:5-10

"O LORD, how long shall I cry for help, and you will not listen?"

O LORD, how long shall I cry for help, and you will not listen? Or cry to you "Violence!" and you will not save? Why do you make me see wrong-doing and look at trouble? Destruction and violence are before me; strife and contention arise. So the law becomes slack and justice never prevails. (Habakkuk 1:2-4a)

The prophet Habakkuk is thought to have written these verses some twenty-seven hundred years ago. And yet, I could have spoken them myself every day this week, any month this year, or last year, or any year or any month since I started paying attention.

The prophet begins his book with these words that dare to question and complain to God and then goes on to say that he will simply station himself at his watch post and wait to see how God will reply.

Why do you make me look at trouble? Why do you not save your people from violence? I'm going to stand here until you answer me.

This week it was the shooting rampage at a Sikh Temple in Milwaukee. Before that it was the shooting spree at a movie theater in Colorado. Before that it was Seattle. And that was just this summer. Before that, Tucson. Norway. Virginia Tech. The Amish community. Columbine. Selma. Kent State. Vietnam. Gallipoli. Gettysburg....

Those are just a few highlights of some "celebrated" times and places of violence and destruction. In truth, God's people are dying violently every single day and on every continent on Earth, the victims of ethnic cleansing, gangs, civil war, hate, poverty, and domestic violence. The front page of the newspaper shows me this kind of news every day, and there are many more stories that never even make the paper.

It's enough to make one question one's faith. Justice never prevails, complains the prophet—and what is justice anyway, I wonder? Revenge means more violence and hatred. Does more killing somehow even things out? If justice means making things right again, well, how does that happen? After all the blood and hate, after the shots are fired or the mosque is burned or the woman is violated in front of her children or the little girl is shot by a stray bullet in her drug-infested neighborhood, how can anything ever be made right again?

And so Habakkuk cries out to God, and sometimes so do I. If you want me to believe in you, if you want me to have faith, then why do you make me look at all this? Why don't you do something?

God's answer to Habakkuk was a command to write God's vision in big letters out there in the world so that everybody could see it. For there is still a vision, despite all this, says God. Wait for it, for it will surely come. Remember God's promises. Remember that God is faithful. Remember that God hears the cries of God's people and that God has stretched out a mighty arm to save, not once but many times. Remember the stories of God and keep faith.

The world has its ways. And they are ways of violence and destruction, of lies and deceit, of the needy being sold for a pair of sandals (to quote another prophet, Amos). The world's ways are death-dealing ways, and we see them played out every day, in the papers, and in our schools and offices, on television and at the movies, and on our streets.

But God's ways are different. God's ways are life-giving. God's ways turn water into an overflowing abundance of wine, and give sight to the blind, and strength to the failing, and love to those whom the world casts aside. God's ways result in the lame man dancing away from a life of shame and poverty. God's ways show kindness to the stranger, and generosity to the alien, and compassion and healing care for the ones left for dead by the side of the road.

And we are called to bear witness to God's ways, in lives lived out loud and in big letters, so that everyone can see. We are called to bear witness in the midst of death and destruction—for where else does it have real meaning?—to God's ways of peace and justice, and right relationship and kindness, and generosity and healing, and love that is not afraid and is stronger than death. We are called to speak out the truth when justice does not prevail, when the poor are once again sold for yet another pair of sandals. We are called to live out God's life-giving vision in our own communities, and to live it large, in the midst of the world and its death-dealing ways.

Because the world needs to see God's vision. It sees that other vision plenty, the vision of sorrow and brokenness, of violence, of screams of terror and the hot tears of grief. It is up to us to make God's life-giving vision plain, to remember the promises and to hold out hope.

For some of us, that means developing the eyes to see God's hand at work in the world around us. God is at work here and now, but many times we are more attuned to the world's work rather than God's. We have to train ourselves to look and see beauty, to see kindness to the friendless, to take note of generosity to the alien and stranger, to see justice lived out, to see peace being made and kept. That training requires us to re-ignite our imaginations and spend time in wonder and awe.

And then, we must find a way to get out of our comfort zones so that we can join God in that work in our world. That's how we bear witness to God's vision, by participating in God's work of love and kindness and peace and justice and generosity, wherever we are. We don't have to go to Africa or live in a monastery or be ordained or certified to do that. We are called to join in God's work in our world, here and now.

There may well still be heartbreak involved. Pulling left-for-dead people out of the ditch, physically or metaphorically, is not for the faint of heart. Standing up for the scapegoat-of-the-week and calling the world to account is going to make us break a sweat. But the world needs to see us, as followers of Jesus, with our arms reaching out in love without fear, living large that vision of God's smack in the middle of what otherwise would threaten to crush the life out of everything.

So, write the vision. Show the world what God is like in the midst of all that mess that is not God. Hold out the hope of redemption and wholeness to a world that staggers under the weight of its trouble. Open your eyes and reach out your arms in love, in the name of the Lord our God.

2 Kings 5:14-17	*"Stand up and go; your faith*
2 Tim. 2:8-13	
Luke 17: 11- 19	*has saved you."*

Giving thanks is central to Luke's story of the ten lepers. When they realized they were healed, only one of them began to shout praises to God. He turned back, fell at Jesus' feet and thanked him, expressing gratitude for the healing he received.

We're not sure about the other nine. Perhaps they were too busy celebrating, too eager to get on with their lives, or maybe they simply lacked the faith to see the true significance of what had happened and how it had happened. But one had to go back and pay his respects. He recognized he'd been given a gift and that Jesus had done something remarkable for him. Through his actions, the leper reveals a humble spirit and demonstrates a rare sensitivity to the grace of God.

Key to the story is the realization that something more than mere healing had taken place. The leper was made well (v.19). What Jesus did was to not stop with the curing of the man's leprosy; he provided care for the whole of who the man was.

The Greek verb sozo meaning "to be made well" is used here in the original text. Another translation for that verb is "saved." Salvation, as it is intended, is God's provision for the whole of who we are. Through Jesus, God touched every aspect of this man's life and made it new in every way. He experienced complete transformation through the saving grace of God's love.

God touches our lives too. And God offers us transformation—a healing wellness that reaches deep to our very core. It changes us, frees us, enabling us to be more completely whom God created us to be. As the leper who was suddenly free to run, shout, and express himself genuinely and authentically, we should so too relish this opportunity.

Several years ago I was granted a sabbatical that took my family and me to West Africa, where we lived for several weeks in a rural village in the country of Togo. Though we didn't speak the native language and our French was limited, "Thank you" was easily understood. Regularly when we'd express our thanks for food offered, shelter provided, or the hospitality our African neighbors were so generous to provide, the response we'd get was, "Thanks be to God!" Or, to put it in the vernacular, "Don't thank me, God is the reason for this!" Their faith in God was strong, and though they had very little by U.S. standards, they knew that all they had was a gift from God.

I wonder why I'm so slow to make the connection myself. It's something the one leper in Luke's story picked up on right away and responded to with great enthusiasm. The more I reflect the more I fear I'm more like the other nine, and I'm probably exaggerating to say I notice one tenth of the time!

So what about those other nine? Certainly they knew their skin was healed, but did they know it was an act of God? Did they know that what was being offered was more than physical healing? Did they have any clue of the complete wellness and salvation being handed to them? Apparently, only one saw this salvation for what it was in full, and only one received the gift with gratitude and thanksgiving.

For the gift of God's love given for us, we too have the opportunity to show our appreciation. Thankfulness is a natural response. As Meister Eckhart said, "If in your lifetime the only prayer you offer is thanks, that would suffice." To show appreciation for God and to God is always an appropriate response.

In this way, the leper models faith for us. He goes back to say, "Thank you, God, for what you've done for me." His action helps us to see that gratitude is a key component of faith. His gratitude is shown not to celebrate his own faith, but to show his appreciation for the faith God in Christ has in him! In the end, his gesture is an act of faith itself.

Gratitude is a natural reaction to what God has done and is doing in our lives. But it is not just the words we say. As powerful as the words "thank you" can be, our actions always speak louder. Therefore our prayer of thanks should include the way we live our lives. The leper went back, threw himself down at Jesus' feet in an act of reverence and devotion.

What a surprising thing for him to do! And it's made even more surprising when you consider that he was a Samaritan. Samaritans were outsiders, ritually unclean, the enemy, foreigners who were at odds with the Jewish community. Under normal circumstances, the two didn't get along or even speak to each other. And so, this Samaritan is an unlikely model of faith.

Though an outsider and a stranger to Jewish ritual and practice, he was still able to have faith and act on it. In fact, his ability to do so tells us something important about faith: Faith shouldn't be narrowly defined as a set of beliefs or religious practices. It's not correct dogma or right ritual that defines faith in this context, but relationship!

The Samaritan, by way of his turning to Jesus, enters into relationship with him. He draws near, prostrates himself and thanks the new-found

Lord of his life. He connects with God through him and relates in response to Jesus' helping hand.

Faith, as revealed through this one, isn't about believing the right thing or professing the right creed, but about complete devotion and commitment to the relationship. Such is at the heart of the great commandment to love one another. Which is why Jesus sent him on his way. Love isn't meant to be insular or narrow, but rather outward and like the universe, ever expanding. So Jesus sent him on his way to love and to serve.

The Samaritan in our text for today got it right. He accepted what was offered and responded with thanks. He drew near to God in praise and thanksgiving, and he went forth a changed man to live a new life of gratitude devoted to God and others. It's likely many came to know God through him. And that's what it's really all about, isn't it? Others knowing the same love we do? Living in gratitude for who God is and for what God is doing in our lives.

The question for us today is, will we do the same? Will we respond in kind? Will we live our lives as if our relationship with God matters? Will our lives reflect the same fidelity and devotion as the tenth leper? Will we express our gratitude completely? Maybe, just maybe, Jesus' words to the tenth leper are for us as well. "Get up and go on your way. Your faith—your relationship with me—has made you well."

Now that's something to be thankful for! Amen.

EXOD. 17:8-13
2 TIM. 3:14-4.2
LUKE 18:1-8

"Pay attention to what the dishonest judge says."

It was the annual celebration at the Cathedral for those married twenty-five or fifty years. The bishop had singled out a Golden Jubilarian, Luigi, asking him to take a few minutes to come up to the microphone and share some insight into how he managed to stay married to the same woman all these years. Luigi said to the congregation, "Well, I've a tried to treat her well, spend-a the money on her, but da best-a is-a dat I took her to Italy for the twentieth anniversary." The bishop immediately commented, "Luigi, you are an amazing inspiration to all the husbands here. Please tell the people what you are planning for your wife for your fiftieth anniversary." Luigi proudly replied, "I'm-a gonna go and a-get her."

Well, neither the bishop nor we expected that! We can picture the bishop coughing and two hefty monsignors quickly hustling Luigi from the sanctuary.

But there's a point to the story, namely, its unexpected twist, the precise mechanism needed to unlock today's puzzling gospel with its challenging parable. So put the story aside and open your hearts.

You heard the gospel: A proud judge who feared no one, neither God nor man, is unwilling to hear the pleas of a poor and defenseless widow, one without a man, without protection, without status. But she persists until she gets justice and the judge gives in, not out of principle, but because he fears the woman will get violent. It is interesting to note, by the way, that in the original language, when the judge says to himself, "I shall deliver a just decision for her, lest she finally come and strike me" the words colloquially mean, "lest she come and give me a black eye!" or, as we would say, "lest she come and punch me out!" Jesus' audience must have chuckled at that line.

In any case, I suspect that all over Catholic Land today, having read this gospel, preachers will be comparing the judge to God and urging the faithful, who are compared to the widow, to be similarly persistent in prayer and not give up. I don't know. I have reservations. This equating the judge with God is very shaky. After all, the Bible is full of lines saying that God hears the cry of the poor, that God is eager and willing to give good things to those who ask. So it's hard, when you really look at it, to equate the insensitive judge with God.

In fact, the storyline says twice that the judge is not exactly a sterling character, for he neither "fears God nor respects man." And besides, is the message that if you badger God long enough you can eventually wear God down and get what you want? Is it right to make God a punchy old man who needs his sleep and if you play your radio loud enough he'll give in? Is the parable saying that you can bribe or bargain with God? And it really doesn't do any good to go through the back door and say, well, the point is that if an insensitive clod of a judge will finally answer the widow's plea, how much more will God? But that too, I think, is straining the comparison.

I suggest that there is a more fruitful and less obvious—and unexpected—way to understand this gospel. Why not see the widow as the image of God, not the judge? Once you reverse characters, then a whole new perspective emerges. That is to say, that when the widow is seen as a God-like figure, then the message of the parable becomes crystal clear: Anyone who determinedly resists injustice, faces it, names it, and denounces it until right is achieved, is acting as God does, is God-like.

Powerless as Jesus on the cross who defeats the power of death, the widow achieves victory for right. Through her persistence the widow becomes a kind of Gandhi or Martin Luther King figure. Against all odds she will endure until justice is done and God will be present.

So the parable is not about strategies to wear down a reluctant God with non-stop prayer or threatening black eyes, but it's about justice, about us little people who act like God whenever we persistently seek, often against terrible odds, to have justice done; whenever—to update the story—we hold self-serving politician's feet to the fire, work to have children insured and free of violence, uncover the greed and corruption that siphons off money from the poor, improve education, and break down barriers that separate people.

A black man and his family were traveling through the South in the 1950s. They stopped to rest a few moments at a park along the highway. His daughters spotted a swing set on a playground in the park and pulled their father toward the swing. They were too young to read the signs that warned that this playground was for "whites only." Sadly but patiently the man told his daughters that they could not play there and explained why. This was their first encounter with racism and they burst into tears. So, much as his mother had done for him when he was a child, the man gathered his children into a warm embrace and said to them "Listen, you little girls are somebody. In fact, you are so important and so valuable to God and so powerful that it takes the governor, the lieutenant governor, and the whole state police force to keep you girls off those swings."

One day because another widow named Rosa Parks would persist, those girls would grow up to see justice done and the signs taken down and God would be present.

So, once more, the judge is anyone who thwarts justice and the woman of our gospel is anyone who acts like God in her pursuit of justice.

This woman is formidable. I wonder though: Was she the only one to take on the judge, the only one to hunger and thirst for justice? She shouldn't be. She should have us for company. And that's what this gospel is really all about.

Taken from Once Upon a Gospel: Inspiring Homilies and Insightful Reflections *by William J. Bausch (New London, CT: Twenty-Third Publications), 2008.*

SIR. 35:12-14, 16-18
2 TIM. 4:6-8, 16-18
LUKE 18:9-14

"The one who humbles himself will be exalted"

A guy goes to a doctor and the doc says, "You have cancer."

The guy rather indignantly replies, "I want a second opinion."

"Okay. You're ugly, too."

The joke works, in part, on the age old mischief of comparison. Some are taller, better looking, smarter than others. Some are short, cosmetically challenged, and a few French fries short of a Happy Meal. My old spiritual director in the novitiate, Fr. Henry Haske, used to tell us novices, "Comparisons are odious."

Today Jesus tells the parable of the Pharisee and the Publican. Jesus is showing that comparing ourselves to others in a game of "I'm up because you're down" is not the way of those baptized into the body of Christ. As baptized, we are in relation with one another as brothers and sisters, not as competitors. Sibling rivalry, "You were Mom's favorite," or "Marcia, Marcia, Marcia," has no place in Christian community.

The Lord is a God of Justice. God rights relationships. That's what justice is, i.e., the righting of relationships, getting relationships right.

This is a shocking parable because it inverts the relationships of the expected social order. The Pharisees were respected religious personages.

The publicans were corrupt minor officials who collected taxes for the Roman oppressors. Tax collectors demanded more than the Romans called for and then pocketed the difference. Good work if one could get it, and could stomach oppressing members of one's own community. Tax collectors were hated and despised. Yet it's the tax collector who leaves the place of prayer "justified," i.e., put "right" with God.

It would be like a Cardinal praying in his cathedral and looking down on a Sister from an LWCR congregation, telling God how much better he is than the Sister, as she humbly begs God for help. Or a CEO of a major corporation blowing his own horn before God and looking down on the janitor who humbly asks for help putting groceries on the table for his children. In such a parable, both the sister and the janitor would go away justified, i.e., in right relationship, with God. The Cardinal and the CEO would have "missed the mark," the literal translation of the word for sin (*harmatia*) in the New Testament.

"Holding others in contempt" is the real kicker in this parable. Delusions of grandeur are bad enough. It's thinking that others merit or deserve one's contempt that really ticks off Jesus. We cannot be right with God if we're walking around mentally comparing ourselves to others in ways that make them come up short. We're called to love, cherish and serve one another, not put one another down.

We all know someone who thinks their "stuff" doesn't stink. It's amusing to hear such persons disparage the drug addict or "welfare queen." As if the John Edwards, Tiger Woods and Lindsay Lohans of the world don't exist. Rich and poor, educated and uneducated, ghetto resident or gated community denizen, let's not forget: we have all sinned and fallen short of the glory of God (cf. Romans 3:23). Looking honestly at ourselves makes us humble.

To practice humility is not to beat ourselves up about shortcomings. God knows most of us have plenty about which to be ashamed. Mark Twain once said, "Man is the only animal that blushes. Or needs to."

The word humility comes from the Latin *humus* meaning earth or dirt. Humility means we are grounded. We are dust and to dust we shall return. We are instructed to do justice, love tenderly, and walk humbly with God (cf. Micah 6:8), not to make it to the cover of *Newsweek* or win some prize on a "reality TV" show. "Reality TV." There's an oxymoron if there ever as one. And there I go, falling into the same trap which I'm preaching against! Putting something down to try and put something else up.

Humility is, ultimately, honesty. To be humble means to neither exaggerate nor minimize, but to accept what is (cf., Kurtz and Ketcham, 1992, *The Spirituality of Imperfection*, p. 187).

Real spirituality, real prayer, focuses us and helps us see clearly what is, not what we think ought to be, not what we want "X," "Y," or "Z" to be, but what actually is. *Everything Belongs* by Fr. Richard Rohr is the best book I ever read on prayer. He writes, "Prayer is not 'one of ten thousand things.' It's that by which we see ten thousand things" (2003, p. 93).

We often fear seeing and knowing things, people, processes and relationships as they really are. To see things as they are may call us to change.

That's the risk of prayer. When we really pray, we stop telling God how good or bad we are. We pay more attention to God's whisperings in our lives and start listening ("silent" and "listen" are spelled with the same letters!). God calls us to conversion and transformation. God takes us up on the invitation to get involved in our lives. And when that happens, the adventure begins.

Real prayer, humble and honest prayer, changes what we desire. We begin to want the transformation promised us by God. We yearn to "come to share in the divine nature" (II Peter 1:4. NAB). God is transforming all of us, all of creation, all of human history (Rom 8:21) into the Kingdom of God. *Lumen Gentium*, Vatican II's profound description of the Church, says God's plan is "to dignify men and women with a participation in His own divine life" (*Lumen Gentium*, 2). This isn't some radical, unorthodox, crazy, Jesuit spin on spirituality. "For the Son of God became Man so that we might become God" (St Athanasius, *Catechism of the Catholic Church*, #460). Prayer makes us aware of, and committed to, this transformation in Christ.

All prayer is relational. By praying, we relate to God and then God relates to us through the choices of our lives. As Dumbledore told Harry, "It is our choices that show what we truly are, far more than our abilities" (Rowling, 1999, *Harry Potter and the Chamber of Secrets*, p. 333).

God calls us to love. Prayer encourages us to make the tough choices love entails. Prayer gives grace, i.e., the power, to do what God asks of us. Love is "the disciplined generosity we require of ourselves when we would rather be selfish" (Carter, 2002, *The Emperor of Ocean Park*, p. 215). The parent of a child suffering from cystic fibrosis must thump the child on the back at night to help the youngster breathe. It hurts the kid, and hurts the adult who must do the thumping. Aging parents call adult children to make hard, loving choices to take the car keys or move mom or dad into a nursing home. Parents of recalcitrant teens know how hard and gut wrenching and infuriating it can be dealing with a fifteen year old "know it all." Such parents love and pray, and pray hard! Knowing the poor in our town go hungry may inspire someone to really love by donating time, talent and treasure to a local soup kitchen.

So let's stop comparing and let's start choosing to love. And to help us do that, let us pray.

"Today salvation has come to this house"

O*ne of my favorite readings* in all of the Old Testament is the first reading today, taken from the 11th and 12th chapters of the Book of Wisdom. It's one of those early promises of what we eventually understand as universalism: God's love toward all without exception.

"You have mercy on everything because you can do everything. You overlook all of our sins. You love everything that you have made. You loathe nothing that you have made. If you had hated it, why would you have made it? How can a thing remain in existence unless you want it to or be preserved had it not been called forth by you? You spare all things because all things are yours, oh Lord, lover of life. Your imperishable spirit is in everything."

Hidden away, this passage is a jewel that becomes much of Jesus' world view which is illustrated in this marvelous gospel. Notice it starts by saying that Jesus intends to pass through and that's actually repeated a second time. Jericho is the suburban rich people's getaway from Jerusalem, so Jesus doesn't expect anybody in Jericho to listen to him or know what he's talking about. In most of human history, before capitalism, people assumed that there was a limited amount of capital. There was only so much to go around. There was no idea of increasing it. There simply is what there is. The assumption was that if you're rich, you have always taken advantage of someone else. To be rich meant you had literally taken from the poor. This very strong bias against rich people is reflected in the entire Bible and certainly in the teaching of Jesus.

So this gospel passage goes out of its way to show that this man was one of those who benefited from the Roman occupation. He was the chief tax collector and a wealthy man in this town of wealthy people. But you might say, without just playing on the word too much, he went out on a limb. He did so by putting himself in a position where he could see, possibly out of spiritual curiosity. It seems that although he was a rich man, he was also humble enough to lose his dignity and to climb up in the sycamore tree. And as we often read, Jesus takes the initiative. Jesus notices him and knows his name.

Now, the name Zacchaeus literally means 'the pure one.' So, maybe Jesus is playing on that name, we're not sure, but he calls him by name. No doubt Zacchaeus was surprised that Jesus would even know his name and much less invite himself to stay at Zacchaeus' house! Maybe this is a metaphor for how religious encounter often happens. All we can do is place ourself in a position of openness, desire, curiosity, and God does all the rest. Here we have Jesus taking the initiative, saying I'm going to come into your world because you put yourself out, just a little bit, to enter into mine.

So, we have the rich man who is assumed to be a sinner and we have the good law-abiding Jews, maybe even the disciples taking offense. I can't think of a single passage in the New Testament where people take offense and it doesn't reveal their own problem. People who take offense are usually proud people, usually arrogant people, usually judgmental people, and I'm sad to say, very often religious people. Religious people just love to take offense. But the part of you that takes offense is not your soul. It is not God within you. God doesn't take offense. As the first reading said,

God loves everything that is. It would not persist being if God did not, on some level, love it and accept it. Thus we are all called to move to that level of 'God seeing' to stop taking offense at things and just say, 'it is what it is.' If God is allowing it, what does this moment, what does this person, what does this situation have to teach me?

So Jesus goes to stay at the house of the sinner. I guess some religious people today would say he's cooperating, he's encouraging, he's complicit. But we see Zacchaeus standing up to the challenge and saying yes, I might be a rich man but I am also a just man. And this is the break-through in this passage. That riches in themselves maybe are not evil as long as you are just. And that's, of course, the word that still needs to be heard. If we do have more than we deserve of this earth's possessions, the least we can do, the best we can do is give some of it away. And we see Zacchaeus going way beyond what is expected – four times over he will repay if he had ever extorted from anybody. And Jesus responds to him, without any further orthodoxy tests or morality tests, "Today salvation has come to this house. You are a rich man, but you are also a just man, and you're not just a just man, but you are a generous man." So justice and generosity become, in this passage, the very name of salvation.

And Jesus ends, as he often does, by saying that he didn't come to create a country club of nice people. He didn't come for the good. He came for those who are lost." This becomes Jesus' statement of his desire and of God's desire for universal salvation. And furthermore a recognition that sometimes those who are on the outside are really on the inside and those of us who think we're on the inside maybe aren't at all.

2 MACC. 7:1-2, 9-14
2 THESS. 2:16 – 3:5
LUKE 20:27-38

"The Lord is not God of the dead, but of the living."

This sort of strange Gospel clearly illustrates what have been the two parallel belief systems in all the religions of the world, and is reflected in Judaism between the Pharisees and Sadducees. One side believed that life lasts forever and another side argued that this is the only life and then it's over. We, from the Christian tradition, so take it for granted that life is eternal because that's what Jesus believed. But in fact that has not been the case with much of the world and it's still not the case.

It's sort of surprising to most of us. But the question is when is the real life? Is the real life now? Is the real life later? Or is it something else? Those who believe that the real life is now, we would probably call them atheist or materialist. In Jesus' own lifetime the group that didn't believe the real life is now were called the Sadducees and it was one-half of the Jewish people. They were divided into two groups, sort of like Catholics and Protestants. They had Sadducees and Pharisees. The Sadducees believed that this life was it and it's over. The Pharisees believed, as Jesus did, in eternal life.

Often the first reading of this Sunday gets a great deal of attention because it has a bit of torture and gore. It gives us some first hints in Judaism that there might be such a thing as eternal life as we read of these young boys being killed and believing that in fact they will live forever—a promise and a hope.

So what is the question? Is the real life just now? Frankly, those who believe that the real life is just now tend to take this life much more seriously.

One evening my Jewish friends had me over for dinner. After the meal one of them said, "You know, we don't believe in eternal life." But yet these people were some of the most dedicated people to the poor, to social change, to making this world a better place because they didn't believe it was some reward punishment system for later. It was all about *now*. And about being a true *mensch*, as they put it—a true human being, which in itself was its own reward. I think we have a lot to learn from that because many of us have put off the real life into the next world.

Frankly, an awful lot of Christians don't take this life very seriously at all. When you see how we've treated the earth, how we've treated one another, how we've killed one another in war almost non-stop in Christian history, you realize that we don't take this world very seriously at all. But, there is a downside to totally believing that the real life is in the next world. Both belief systems have their pluses and minuses. What, therefore, might the Gospel be?

I think the Gospel, and it's revealed in this somewhat abstruse saying of Jesus, is that the real life is both now *and* then and how you do it now is how it will be forever. Brothers and sisters, God only gives you exactly what you want, that's all. It's really very simple, and your life right now is saying what you want. If you want a life of negativity, of separation, of judgments, of hatred, that's Hell and it begins right now. And there are people right now I'm afraid even reading this homily who are living in Hell. They're not going to be surprised. God just gives you what you want and it's basically non-existence. Not to love is not to live. Not to love is not to live forever. Some people choose non-existence. Some people choose hatred and Hell.

If you're choosing love then you're choosing the eternal element that exists forever. If you're choosing to love and serve this world and your neighbor, you're already in Heaven. Maybe it doesn't always feel like that but in fact it's the foretaste of the promise. And Jesus isn't putting down marriage in this reading. He's simply saying marriage is a school of eternity because at least you're learning how to be united to one other person. But the reason he says Heaven will not be about marriage is because Heaven is a universal connection not just with one other person but with everything and everybody.

Everything you have loved will be with you in eternity. Many of us will be happy to know that includes our dog or our cats. If you have never loved anything you have no Heaven to go to. If you've hated every day for a different reason you'll be at home in Hell. That's what you've chosen. You like to be separate, negative, cantankerous and oppositional. Brothers and sisters don't make that mistake, but it all is about *now*. As now, so forever. The best one liner that I've quoted for years is from St. Catherine of Siena. She says, "It's Heaven all the way to Heaven and it's Hell all the way to Hell."

33RD SUNDAY IN ORDINARY TIME

REV. PENNY A. NASH

MAL. 3:19-20A
2 THESS. 3:7-12
LUKE 21:5-19

"You know how one must imitate us."

I don't know about you, but I tend to get a little anxious when Jesus starts talking about wars and insurrections and false messiahs and the destruction of the Temple, and how our relatives are going to betray us to the authorities.

And sometimes I get confused when Paul announces what sounds like a mandate to close down all the soup kitchens and food pantries, making me wonder if he even knew the story of the feeding of the 5,000 after all, or if we should all take our contributions back from the local food pantry, not to mention cancel our harvest basket programs.

There has to be some context here! And, of course there is.

Once upon a time there was a young church in Thessaloniki, the Roman capital of Macedonia, a church that Paul had planted and to whom he wrote the very first letter we have in the whole New Testament only twenty or so years after Jesus' death.

The folks in this community were particularly concerned about the second coming of Christ. This was a great expectation of the Thessalonians, and probably all of the early Christian communities; in Paul's first letter to them, he goes to some length to explain and reassure them that their relatives and friends who have died will still be part of the great resurrection when Jesus returns. They really don't need to worry about that.

But meanwhile they do need to worry about doing their work within the community and setting a good example. Paul himself set a good example, working night and day, he says. The Thessalonians don't want to be considered some kind of odd sect, he suggests, but they do apparently keep to themselves, so that they do not depend on the outside world.

It seems, however, that at least some of the Thessalonians decided that since Jesus was going to come back any minute anyway, and since they were all saved anyway, then they would just sit back and wait in leisure, letting others take care of things. And, because in his first letter Paul explained that Jesus would return like a thief in the night (and so they needed to be ready), some of them were compulsively examining every potential clue to see if in fact Jesus is in the process of coming back— could this be a sign? How about that? Is Jesus back yet, is he, is he, is he?

And so Paul had to write a second letter, in which he reiterated several of his points from the first. Perhaps he had overstated the issue about Jesus' imminent return, since time has passed and Jesus still had not come back.

Paul told them pretty much what Jesus says in Luke today: that the gathering of the faithful will not come before there are some big events that are cosmic in scope. It's not going to be subtle. They really won't be able to miss it.

Meanwhile, however, he warned those who are continuing to sit back and wait for the big day without contributing to the community to avoid spending their time getting into everybody's business. And so he called down the slackers, which is where our passage today comes in. We all are to work to build up the community, not to simply wait in leisure for Jesus to come back.

So there's our context.

Paul is not saying that we should not feed the hungry unless they get jobs. That would go against the grain of everything the Old Testament (Paul's

Scriptures) and Jesus (Paul's Lord) are about: caring for the most vulnerable among us, feeding the hungry, clothing the naked, showing hospitality to the resident alien and the traveler. That would be like saying we only assist people who do not need help.

Paul is saying, do your work, don't be a busybody, don't sit around and let others take care of you, don't neglect doing your part in building up the community, just because you're "busy" waiting for Jesus to come and save you personally.

The early Christian communities did tend to keep to themselves. They lived somewhat separate from society and took care of their own. Our world, however, is not very much like the world of first century Roman Macedonia. We do live in the world, and we are not separated like a funny sect. The church has evolved. It has grown beyond tiny communities anxiously searching the heavens for signs of Jesus' return and has over time discerned its call to be his hands and feet in the world, not just inside the church but for the whole community, as far as we can reach, and even beyond our own reach. We are able to do this as part of the larger community of the Church.

While we all know that institutions can spend resources on self-maintenance and even become corrupt, it is also true that through institutions we can deliver many good things to many people. Together, we are stronger than we are alone; together, we can do so much to feed the hungry and clothe the naked and shelter the stranger.

There's great hunger out there; people need to be fed in so many ways. Families trying to escape poverty, addiction, domestic violence, and homelessness need not only food but classes to teach them how to be self-sufficient. There are mentally ill folks who need dinner on Wednesday nights and who also hunger for friendship and community. Homeless people need peanut butter sandwiches and also the human touch provided by those who wash their feet and give them clean socks. Children hunger for relationships with other children from all over the world so that they can learn how much they have in common with people of other faiths instead of learning to demonize them. Women in poverty hunger for the means to feed their families and become productive members of their communities.

And so, our context (unlike the Thessalonians') is this: We live in a world where people are hungry, suffering from hunger of every kind. And Jesus says, whatever you do to the least of these, you do to me. Let's not sit back and wait for Jesus our personal savior to make things better.

Let's work together to make our world better in his name.

FEAST DAYS

Prov. 8:22-31	*"The Spirit of truth will*
Rom. 5:1-5	
John 16:12-15	*guide you to all truth"*

Two decades ago, I attended a fundamentalist Bible college in Chicago and studied to be a missionary. I've strayed from my initial beliefs, but I'm trying to look back and figure out what I appreciate about my experience. One of the main things that I value is that people had an incredible range of ways in which they could connect with God.

For instance, I worked in Cabrini Green each week. At the time, Cabrini was the most violent inner-city neighborhood in the United States. So I would spend afternoons playing basketball, jumping rope, and teaching Bible stories. I don't think the children learned much from me. I would prepare my lessons from the suburban white kid curriculum, and ask them questions about stealing a cookie from the cookie jar, when they were telling me about how their friend got busted for bringing a gun to class. I think the greatest service I provided for them was just hanging out and keeping them busy with something to do after school.

I learned a lot though. I found out what the gangs would permit them to wear to school—certain colors or shoes were not allowed. One time, as I was riding on a bus, we passed this lush beautiful lawn. I asked the little girl next to me why there weren't any children playing there. She explained that everyone knew the field was used for target practice. They would be shot if they played on that field. I looked down at her little knees, wondering what it would be like to live in a place where your neighbors would shoot you if you stopped to enjoy the grass.

At the same time, I studied to become a missionary, learning basic skills about how to communicate in a particular context. We learned how to observe a culture, understand its patterns, rituals, and power dynamics. I learned how to write down a language phonetically, so that if I went to a tribe in Africa that only had an oral language, I could learn it, transcribe it, and translate the Bible into their language.

I learned that words were not the only things that needed to be translated. Even though the people who surrounded me took the Bible literally, we were instructed to change the phrases of Scripture. My teacher would explain, "If you're in an African tribe, and you're trying to explain how sins have become white as snow, that will not work. People have not seen or experienced snow. Find something pure in their culture and use that word instead."

One day, our Cross-Cultural Ministries professor explained to the class, "If you are working with children in Cabrini Green, you should not refer to God as Father." He quoted a statistic, pointing out that the neighborhood was matriarchal in nature. The mother was the sole caretaker in most of the homes. And when we constantly referred to God as Father, it could have negative connotations for the children growing up in these homes. "It would be better if you spoke about God as a Mother who cannot ignore her nursing child," he explained, quoting a verse from Isaiah 49.

I still find it strange that I learned all of this in a Bible college. It was certainly not the hotbed of feminist thought. But they were concerned with making sure that the story of Jesus made sense in a particular context.

The doctrine of the Trinity works in the same way. On one hand, the doctrine is rich and complex as we try to fully comprehend it. On the other hand, it has a simplicity that allows us to connect and commune with

God in the way that makes the most sense. The ease and accessibility of the Trinity allows us to understanding God in powerful ways.

For some people, looking at creation and knowing that there is a God who delights in crafting the smallest flower that will whither in a day or the deep sea fish that will never be seen by a human eye is enough to inspire them. The idea of God the Creator forming us in God's image gives meaning to one of the core questions in life: "Why do I exist?" The knowledge that we live because we have been created by the divine, that we are formed in God's image for a reason and a purpose brings meaning to each day.

Another person might be inspired by the wisdom of Jesus. We memorize the words, allowing his teachings to become a part of our daily rhythm. We appreciate the man of sorrows who knows how to weep and walk alongside us in our pain. To hear how God journeyed among us, partaking in a sacred meal, suffering the depths of human emotion, gives people a sense of unity with the divine. Having someone who has gone before us, who knows what we might be feeling, allows us a sense that someone understands.

And for others, to have a Spirit who will not leave us abandoned and neglected, but fills us with abundance and joy, allows another path of communion with the divine. The Spirit moves in and among us, enlightening us, aiding our intellect, and helping us to fathom the mysteries surrounding us. The Spirit whispers understanding in our most confusing times and gives meaning to our deepest groaning. The Spirit of God gives birth to us, even as we give birth. We create alongside God. That powerful force of creation allowed us a glimpse of who God is, so much so that many Christians describe themselves as being born-again.

God is one substance, three persons, and many names. May we live each day with anticipation of how God might reveal God's self to us in new ways.

To the glory of God our Creator, God our Liberator, and God our Sustainer. Amen.

GEN. 14:18-20
1 COR. 11:23-26
LUKE 9:11B-17

"This is my body that is for you."

Recently I was back to my alma mater, Fordham University. While visiting I was reminded of a Jesuit, Walter Ciszek, who died there on the feast of the Immaculate Conception, in 1984 and who had a profound influence on my life. Recently the Vatican gave its formal approval for the canonization process for Walter Ciszek and he will probably be canonized a saint one day. He wrote two books: *With God in Russia* and *He Leadeth Me.* For those of you who like to do spiritual reading I would urge you to read these books, for they were a profound grace for me as a young man.

Walter Ciszek was born in Pennsylvania. While in the seminary, the Holy Father was asking for some who might go east to places like Poland and Walter volunteered. When he went there he had no idea of what was going to happen, as Poland had recently been divided in two—the Nazi and Soviet territories. Fortunately or unfortunately, he was caught behind the lines in the Soviet District and thought he would go unnoticed. But because of his promise to the Holy Father he said he would stay there and help the people. But it was not too long before he arrested by the Soviets as a spy for the Vatican. While they never admitted that they were holding him as a spy, for the next five years Walter Ciszek never saw a human face, never heard a human voice, except for those of his interrogators.

Finally, after five years, he signed a false confession, which he wrote was the worst time of his life. He thought he sold out God, his Church, and his country. He was sent from Lubianka to the terrible prison system of Gulag. While in that prison system, he prayed, asking how he could best find God. For five years he never said Mass. As time went on eventually some nuns would smuggle some bread and wine into that prison. The first Mass he said was actually under the cover of his cot. Knowing he was alone and that the Eucharist is not supposed to be for "just me" he decided to ask some if they would like to go to Mass, knowing if they got caught they would be killed.

In those days you fasted from midnight until the next day when you received Communion and even though they probably didn't have to, they decided they would receive only after fasting. They were fed only two meals of gruel a day; morning and evening. Walter decided that the best time to say Mass would be at noontime when the guards would go eat and leave the prisoners to fall down and rest. So Walter would take them deeper into the woods or the salt mines and they would celebrate Mass and receive the Eucharist. Every one of them would not eat the morning gruel and they would fast from the midnight before. Sometimes the guards would come by and they could not say Mass at noontime. So they had an option: no Mass, no Eucharist or perhaps wait till that night and try to sneak off together to say Mass. If they did that it meant no supper, meaning 36 hours without eating in a concentration camp. And they would do it. The desire for Eucharist was so strong that they would forgo nourishment just to receive the Eucharist.

So today we celebrate the feast of the Most Holy Body and Blood of Christ, also known as Corpus Christi. And we come to celebrate Eucharist. I do not think that many of us give up too many meals. Probably not many are fasting from midnight the night before. Sometimes we do not even fast the hour. It gets kind of simple for us and we take it for granted. It is so easy. We can receive Communion every day, and some of you do. We can receive every weekend, and most of you do. I hope to God that it is never just "a thing to do." You see, the Walter Ciszek and unnamed martyrs and saints of the past—they would be hurt.

So I ask us to renew our deep, deep faith in the Eucharist. So that when we do come, we come in thanksgiving. We come knowing what Christ has given us. We come to appreciate that the Eucharist itself forgives as well as it is forgiving. We come to receive Eucharist so that you and I can become Eucharist. It doesn't stop at the altar rail—it just begins. When we leave Church we should know that we are Eucharist to others.

With God in Russia—well, maybe one of you can write a book *With God in…* "whatever your hometown is." And maybe we can be a sign to so many others that we believe, we do, and we are because of what God has given us.

FEAST OF ALL SAINTS

JAMES MARTIN, S.J.

Rev. 7:2-4, 9-14
1 John 3:1-3
Matt. 5:1-12

"Rejoice and be glad, for your reward will be great in heaven"

Recently I was given a wonderful gift. And since it wasn't cash, I didn't have to hand it in to the Jesuits! Actually, it was something of a spiritual gift, so I can share it with you today.

There is a Jesuit church in New York City called St. Francis Xavier, named after the 16th-century Jesuit missionary. If you've ever been in the church, you'll know that it's dark inside. Well, no, that's not true—it's very dark. Decades of grimy soot from passing cars, smoke from thousands of candles and countless grains of incense, and a very high ceiling that was probably never well lit, all made it a gloomy place. You could barely see the ceiling.

Well, no longer. Last summer the marble was cleaned, the mosaics were washed, the brass polished, the stained glass restored, and the pews replaced. The church has been renewing itself. And ever since I heard about the project, I was dying to peek in to see what it was like.

For one thing, I hoped that the saints would be easier to see. The church has all these wonderful statues of the saints. But the saints are perched high above the congregation, and in the gloom you could barely see them. And way in the back of the church, in the apse, so high that you can barely see them, are five saints, larger than the rest. And I never knew who they were; the saints seemed so far away.

Anyway, last week I was visiting a Jesuit priest who lives there, for dinner. "If you come early," he said, maybe we could get into the church." Providentially, we ran into the pastor and he pointed us to a side door, which opened into the interior of the church, which was completely empty, and completely quiet.

It was breathtaking. The newly cleaned church glows with glorious colors: whites and creams and yellows and golds. And the first thing I saw, perched above the aisles on both side, were the gleaming white statues of the saints. The church had made it easier to see them.

"But oh," my friend said, "we have to climb up the scaffolding. I want to show you something."

Now, the whole back half of the church was completely filled with metal scaffolding from floor to ceiling. So we ducked under the intricate framework and stepped onto a staircase, which was the reason they coined the word "rickety." When we took that first step the whole staircase shook. "Uh, I don't think so," I said worriedly to my friend. "No, really," he said, "you have to see this." So we started to climb.

Soon we were halfway up the full height of the church and I didn't dare look down or up. "Um, I think this is fine here," I said, somewhat frightened.

"No," he said. "It's worth it."

Just then the pastor came into the church and said, "Hey, you're going up! Let me help," and he turned a switch, flooding the space with light.

We kept climbing, and soon I saw the underside of a wooden floor above us. We got closer and I poked my head through a little opening in the floor.

When we emerged into the small space, I was amazed. We were in the very rear of the church, way up in the apse, in front of those five saints that had always seemed not only so small, but so far away. Impossibly high. And we were only a few feet away from the ceiling of the church, glowing in yellows and golds. Now I could see clearly see the life-sized saints, who stood silently, right before us: St. Ignatius Loyola, St. Francis Xavier, and St. Joseph. Towards the center was Mary. And in the very center was Jesus.

It was hard to say why it was so moving, so "consoling", as St. Ignatius would say. Maybe because of the sheer beauty. Maybe because I was so close to the statues of five people who I love. Maybe because I remembered a line from the "vow formula" that we Jesuits pronounce, about standing before the "entire heavenly court." Maybe all those things.

It dawned on me that the Christian journey is something like this climb. Of course today is the Feast of All Saints. And sometimes the saints can seem to us like their statues are in many churches: obscure, hard to identify, far off. But when you get to know them, by learning more about their real lives, your vision changes: you see them clearly, and you see how close their lives can be to yours, if you're willing to begin that climb.

Something similar happened in my own church, the Church of St. Ignatius Loyola, a little further uptown in New York. In the rear of the church is a lovely altar dedicated to three young Jesuit saints. And last year, when the marble was cleaned and the brass polished, that marble altar just beamed, it was easier to see all three: Aloysius Gonzaga, Stanislaus Kostka and John Berchmans. Each of them had died early, after leading heroic lives. Aloysius, the scion of a wealthy family who renounced his fortune, died at age 23, after becoming infected in his work with plague victims. St. Stanislaus, who was beaten by his brother over his desires to live a more charitable life, walked 450 miles to enter the novitiate, and died at age 18. St. John Berchmans, a model Jesuit who did small things with love, like St. Thérèse of Lisieux, died at age 23.

After the church was cleaned, a parishioner said to me, "You know, I didn't even know those saints were even there!" And I thought, well, that's true for most of us. We can overlook these incredible saints, and forget about their astonishing stories, which is a sad thing. Because underneath the years of grimy forgetfulness lies a great beauty.

But the climb up that long staircase the other day was like the Christian journey in another way, too. Lately I've realized something about Christianity, something you probably figured out long ago: It's hard. I know that sounds obvious but it took me a long time to figure out. When I entered the Jesuits I figured that if I really understood the Gospel, prayed hard, and got my act together—spiritually, psychologically, emotionally—I could live the Christian life with ease. Once I figured it all out, it would become easy, something I wouldn't even have to think about, sort of like riding a bike.

But that's not true all. It's an effort. It takes work. It's hard. Forgiving people is hard. Loving is hard. And, like climbing those steps, it can be frightening, too. Working with the poor can be frightening. Caring for someone who is ill can be scary. And you start to doubt that you'll make it. You think, "I'll never be able to do this. I'll never be able to climb this far." But you can. You can with the help of friends, who urge you on, saying, "Come on, just a little further." You can climb that ladder within the church. You can walk towards Jesus.

And you can climb that ladder with the help of the saints, who encourage you from their posts in heaven, as our patrons and our companions, as our examples, and as those who pray for us. You know, I'm always so happy when churches renew the statues of the saints because the saints do the same thing for the church. One of the old Mass prayers included a magnificent line in praise of God, which says, "You renew the church in every age, by raising up men and women outstanding in holiness."

The saints clean the church with their holiness, coming precisely when we need them most. St. Francis of Assisi comes preaching simplicity when people need relief from corruption and scandal. St. Ignatius of Loyola comes when people need a new way to find God in all things. Mother Teresa comes when we need to be reminded of the call to care for the poor and forgotten.

But it wasn't easy for them either. The saints knew best of all that, like that staircase, the path to God is frightening and can tempt us to doubt. But they knew something else too: it's worth it.

Now, sometimes in our daily life, or in our prayer, we take that path and we feel so close to God. When I was standing in front of those statues, I said to my friend, "You know, we'll never be here again. We'll never get this high again. The scaffolding will come down and we'll only look up at them."

And my friend said, "Don't forget to touch one before you leave." So I reached out and touched the foot of St. Ignatius. And then the hem of the Jesus's robe. And I thought, "Well, I'll think of that the next time I'm in here and look up at them."

How like our lives. We have a deep experience of God, we feel lifted up, or close to the divine, and may not have another experience like that for years. We must look from below, remembering. Think of Mother Teresa, who had a profound spiritual experience early in life, which led her to care for the poor, and then faced silence from God for the rest of her life.

I was thinking about all these things at the top of the ladder. And what is that ladder, exactly? How do we get closer to Jesus, Mary and the saints? How do we travel to God? Well, the ladder is the Beatitudes, today's

Gospel. That's the climb the saints made. Each of those beatitudes is a step on the staircase.

Poverty of Spirit.

Mercy.

Meekness.

Righteousness.

Purity of Heart.

Peacemaking.

And the willingness to suffer persecution.

Each of those steps may seem hard, even dangerous, to step on, and it may seem that we can't do it, but that's the path we're invited to climb. And it's Jesus Christ himself who urges us on, saying, "Come on. It's worth it. I know it looks hard. I know you think you can't do it. I know you think you can't strive for holiness, but you can. Wait till you see what I have in store." And at the end of the climb is something that may seem hard to see, something that God calls us to: sanctity. Blessedness. For blessed are the merciful. Blessed are the peacemakers. Blessedness, sanctity, is God's goal for us. But there is something else waiting for us, something that the saints show us with their lives. And it's something you don't hear much hear about in religious circles: happiness.

For there is another meaning to the word normally translated as "blessed" in the Beatitudes. Makarioi is the original Greek used. And that has another meaning. Happy. So happy are the peacemakers. Happy are the merciful. Happy. Happiness awaits those on the road to sanctity.

So why not step onto the Christian ladder with your eyes fixed on the heavenly court, confident in the prayers of the saints, knowing that you can make it, no matter how difficult or how frightening it may seem? Knowing that, at the end of the climb, both now and in the time to come, you will be near the saints, you will touch Jesus, and you will be blessed.

And happy.

WISD. 3:1-9
ROM. 5:5-11
JOHN 11:28-44

"Untie them and set them free."

For two thousand years this gospel has resonated with the Christian people. The reason is obvious: The same four characters in it are present at every funeral. Let's look. First, there is Lazarus, a beloved family member. We can imagine him slowly wasting away each day. Like those burial bands, he is wrapped tighter and tighter with limitations until, finally, the last band is in place and he is dead.

So it is, was, with our Lazaruses. Outside of a sudden death by accident or heart attack, many of us have witnessed our parents, our spouse, son or daughter or sibling slowly dying. We recall too well the medications, the procedures, the operations, the doctors, the visits, the hospital, hospice; like so many bands, these things are wound round and round until our Lazarus died. It was hard to watch. We felt so helpless. We tried to make the transition easy, but our Lazarus is dead and we are here today with that memory in our hearts.

Then there are Martha and Mary, the grieving relatives. We are they. Now every morning we wake up in an empty bed. Every evening we wrap our arms around the pillow wishing it were him or her, but it's only a pillow and we cry. There is the favorite chair unsat in, the empty place at the dinner table, the loneliness, the ache in the heart. We don't like cooking for one. There is his favorite jacket or her favorite dress. We don't have the heart to throw them out. There is the son or daughter who won't be home any more for Thanksgiving and Christmas, the child who died much too young. Maybe, to add to the burden, there was a suicide and we still, after all these years, have mixed feelings about that. There are, in a word, our tears, grief, memories, and, yes, anger. "If you had been here my brother would not have died. What kind of friend are you?" We feel Martha's anger at God. We'd like to shake a fist, but we're afraid to. We are Martha and Mary.

Next there is the crowd who came to comfort Martha and Mary. Remember, they are the folks who brought food to the house and sandwiches for all after the funeral. They are the ones who sent us Mass cards, called and asked if there was anything they could do. They sympathized with our loss and felt helpless in the face of our grief. Bless them for being there. But when they left, it was lonely.

And finally there is Jesus in the gospel story. He's crying. He isn't crying like our Western males, a trembling lip kept in check, a muffled sob. No, this is a Mideastern Jew of two thousand years ago who, like all his contemporaries, throws his head back and lets out a primal scream. This was his friend, remember, and he loved his friend. But, we note, this Jesus not only has tears, he has compassion. He has pity. He has power that wells up from his love. So Jesus has them bring out the corpse and he prays and he speaks and he dips into his life-giving love and calls out, "Friend Lazarus, come forth." And when Lazarus does, Jesus simply says, "Untie him and set him free."

We are here to remember that Jesus has said the same thing to our Lazarus. "Come forth. Untie him. Untie her. Set them free." And off came the bands: the medication, the intravenous lines, the tubes, the bed, the bandages, the hospital, the restrictions, the depression. And there stands our Lazarus, our Lazarus, free and shinning. Our husband, our wife, our child, our sister, our brother, our mother, our father have known the love-tears of Jesus and the power behind them. They have been untied, freed. The gospel lives once more and we are assembled on this feast of All Souls to affirm it, embrace it, and find comfort in it and remember it.

Yes, we are all here today with memories and prayers, and, if our loss is fresh, with tears. But at this liturgy this gospel, as I said, has been replayed once more. Lazarus, Martha and Mary, friends, and Jesus have again marched across the stage. Lazarus, our loved one, so cherished in memory, Martha and Mary who are us, supporting friends in this congregation, and Jesus, Jesus whose words still echo, "Untie them and set them free."

Taken from Once Upon a Gospel: Inspiring Homilies and Insightful Reflections by William J. Bausch (New London, CT: Twenty-Third Publications), 2008.

2 SAMUEL 5:1-3 COLOSSIANS 1:12-20 LUKE 23:35-43	*"Amen, I say to you, today you will be with me in Paradise"*

In 1925, the world was rebuilding after the end of World War I. Mussolini and fascism were on the rise, our church had lost its political power, having to hole up behind the walls of the Vatican, and the decadence of the Roaring Twenties was off and running. With a strong desire to remind Christians that their allegiance was to their spiritual ruler in heaven as opposed to earthly kings and wealth, Pope Pius XI issued his encyclical Quas Primas, which established the Solemnity of Christ the King, which we celebrate this day. This was Pius' response to the destructive forces of his time, insisting that the only weapon against such military forces and human chaos was the acknowledgment of the sovereignty of Christ.

He said:

> "It is necessary that the royal dignity of Our Lord be recognized and accepted as widely as possible. To this end it seems to us that nothing else would help so effectively as the institution of a special feast dedicated to Christ our King. Documents are often read only by a few learned faithful. But it is the celebration of feasts that can move and teach all the faithful."

In short, the Pope was calling for us to actively participate in the celebration of Christ the King. Simply reading about Christ wasn't enough; we needed to respond and to answer our baptismal call to be a disciple of Christ, to follow Christ, be like our Christ the King.

But that was nearly a century ago, and frankly I am not sure how successful we have been in teaching the faithful and changing humanity. War continues in Iraq and Afghanistan, Sudan still deals with genocide, terrorism threatens global security, the church continues to deal with abuse issues…and the decadence of the Twenties doesn't hold a candle to the Ponzi schemes we have seen over the past decade.

So as we gather to celebrate Christ the King and bring our Liturgical Year to an end, how does this feast teach and move us? What has society missed and not learned over these past years?

Perhaps it is this concept of Kingship. Today there are, no doubt, many false 'kings' that we pay homage to. But look at the kingship that is given to us in today's Gospel. Christ the King reigns from the throne of the cross—a king whose royal crown is made of thorns.

For the whole liturgical year, in our Sunday Gospels, we have followed Christ as seen through the eyes of Luke. Beginning back in January when we began Ordinary Time, Luke gave us the story of Jesus and the first sermon in his home town of Nazareth, where he went into the synagogue, was handed a scroll and proceeded to read from Isaiah, saying:

"The spirit of the Lord is upon me because he has anointed me to bring glad tidings to the poor. He has sent me to proclaim liberty to captives and recovery of sight to the blind, to let the oppressed go free and to proclaim a year acceptable to the Lord."

Jesus immediately applies that passage to himself, identifying himself as the anointed one who will bring God's life changing message of the liberation for the oppressed and the inclusion of the marginalized.

And through the year of Ordinary Time, following Jesus and his journey with his disciples we were treated to story after story of God's love, mercy and forgiveness as Jesus ate with the sinners and the outcasts of society. We heard Luke's story of the repentant prostitute who washed the feet of Jesus with her tears and wiped them with her hair. We heard about the unscrupulous tax collector, Zacchaeus, who was so grateful for Jesus' honoring him with a visit that he promised to become an honest man. We heard the story of the Good Samaritan, who, moved with compassion, was the only one to stop and help the one injured along the side of the road.

God's mercy is expressed in Jesus' table fellowship style of teaching. For Jesus is always eating with new people, the wrong people—women at a men's symposium, non-Jews, and sinners—and ignoring all the purity codes of how, when, and where that his religion required at that time. Christ formed new unity wherever he went. But that new unity requires us to change. It requires us to review our priorities. It requires us to revisit who or what we hold as King in our lives.

This ties into today's gospel story, only told by Luke, of the two thieves being crucified with Christ. With this recounting of the crucifixion of Christ, Luke brings full circle the mission of Christ: the one who was anointed and who proclaimed liberty to the captives, sight to the blind, freedom to the oppressed and who hung on a cross between two thieves. Neither of whom deny their guilt, but only one has the faith to call Jesus by name and who repeats over and over again, "Remember me when you enter your kingdom." It is only the dying and repentant thief who recognizes that this rejected and beaten man is indeed a true king. And even in his agony and pending death Christ shows no anger or vengeance, but assures the penitent thief that he will join him in paradise.

No doubt Pius XI was on the right track in that we need to have a time to celebrate and remember that Christ is our King. But it is something that we need to do every day, not just on this feast day. This whole Liturgical year, we have been given story after story of how Christ demonstrated to us what it means to be his disciple, of how we are called to treat others, of what it means to be Christ to your family, your co-worker, to the people you meet on the street, and to yourself.

And here is the really good news, and it is the part, I think, that we miss and forget the most. We are not perfect and we will fail and we will not always be like Christ and we will not always make the right decisions. And guess what: that is okay.

For look up at that cross—Christ hangs there with his arms outstretched, hanging between two thieves. And, as we heard in our second reading, he holds all things together, forgiving all things, reconciling all things, and loving each of us without conditions.

So as we end this liturgical year, may we remember that Christ's Kingship is not based on "human power", but on loving and serving others, and may we have the faith that allows us to fall into the hands of a living and loving Christ…the Christ who is our King.

THEMATIC CROSS REFERENCE

THE CONTRIBUTORS

REV. WILLIAM J. BAUSCH is a parish priest of the diocese of Trenton, New Jersey. He is the prize- winning author of numerous books on parish ministry, the sacraments, Church history, storytelling and homiletics. His book, *Traditions, Tensions, Transitions in Ministry* received Honorable Mention in 1983 from the Catholic Press Association. *Storytelling: Faith and Imagination* was awarded second place in 1985 for best pastoral work, *The Total Parish Manual* won first place in 1995, *Brave New Church* first place in 2002 and *Once Upon a Gospel* won third place in 2009.

He was awarded the President's Award in 1996 from the National Federation of Priests' Councils for parish leadership, the Catholic Library Association's Aggiornamento Award for Notable Contribution to Parish Life in 2004 and the Walter J. Burghardt, S. J. Preaching Award in 2008 for his contribution to Catholic preaching. He has lectured and given workshops in such colleges and universities as Notre Dame, Sacred Heart in Fairfield, Connecticut, Boston College, Charles Carroll in Cleveland and in most U.S. dioceses as well as abroad. His latest book is *Encounters*, a book of homilies.

First and foremost, however, though retired from the pastorate, he remains happily engaged in his first love: being a parish priest active in assisting at three parishes, writing, and giving lectures and retreats.

JOEL BLUNK is a songwriter, storyteller, truth seeker and soul crafter. For 25 years he's been paying attention to the way truth unfolds in others' lives - on countless football fields, in athletic training rooms and church pews; out in the wilderness; and around the breakfast table. He's worked professionally as an athlete, coach, singer/ songwriter, pastor, and spiritual director. His work now takes form in men's groups, Rites of Passage experiences for youth and young adults, helping older adults embrace the second half of life, caring for the unspoken wounds of returning vets, and tending to the sacred threads that weave one's soul. Joel is the Associate Pastor at the State College Presbyterian Church in central Pennsylvania where he has worked with the Fellowship in Senior High youth group (FISH) for the past 18 years. Today he directs a new outreach known as the WheelHouse http://www.scpresby.org/ which seeks to help people find that place where their "deepest desire and the world's greatest hunger meet." His music is available on iTunes. He loves basketball, playing guitar, hiking with Kristen, and playing disc golf with his three sons.

DOUG CORDES is a freelance graphic designer based in New York City. Originally from Helena, AL, Doug graduated from Auburn University with a BFA in Visual Communications. Doug spent several years in Nashville, TN as a graphic designer for Thomas Nelson Publishers, one of the largest Christian publishing companies in the world. Now, Doug works with authors, artists, and nonprofit companies developing visual identities, book covers and interiors, and web banners.

REV. DR. DAVID A DAVIS is currently the senior pastor of the Nassau Presbyterian Church in Princeton, New Jersey. He has served that congregation since 2000. David earned his Ph.D. in Homiletics from Princeton Theological Seminary. He is currently the Chairperson of the Board of Trustees for the Presbyterian Foundation. His academic work has focused on preaching as a corporate act and the active role of the listener in the preaching event. Before arriving in Princeton, he served for fourteen years as the pastor of the First Presbyterian Church, Blackwood, NJ. David grew up in Pittsburgh and did his undergraduate work at Harvard University where he was a member of the University Choir singing weekly in Memorial Church and listening to the preaching of Professor Peter Gomes. David is married to Cathy Cook, a Presbyterian Minister who is currently Director of Student Relations and Senior Placement at Princeton Seminary. They have two children; Hannah and Ben, both in college.

David is a regular contributor to the *Huffington Post* and various journals in the discipline of preaching and has had published of a collection of his sermons. The book is titled: *A Kingdom You Can Taste: Sermons for the Church Year*.

MICHAEL DOYLE was born on a farm in Rossduff, County Longford, Ireland. Ordained a Catholic priest in Wexford, Ireland he came to the Diocese of Camden in 1959 where he taught high school and assisted in various parishes. In 1974 Msgr. Doyle was appointed pastor of Sacred Heart Parish, where he continues to serve.

Msgr. Doyle earned a Master's Degree in Education from Villanova University in 1962 and received an honorary Doctorate in Humanities from Villanova in May 2007. He has a lifelong commitment to peace and justice. In 1971, he participated in the "Camden 28" peace action against the Vietnam War at the Federal Building in Camden and was arrested. He was acquitted two years later in a trail where he acted as his own defense. Anthony Giacchino directed and produced a documentary about the "Camden 28" in 2007.

He has been the subject of television programs such as *60 Minutes'*, "Michael Doyle's Camden" in 1983; CBS's *Sunday Morning*, December 1995, and of newspaper articles such as *The Philadelphia Inquirer's* series on inspiring preachers, 1996.

During his tenure at Sacred Heart he has established a free medical clinic serving those without medical benefits; founded the Heart of Camden Housing which renovates abandoned houses and assists low-income families to become homeowners and helped to establish Camden Churches Organized for People, CCOP, a church-based community organizing effort. He has written numerous magazine and newspaper articles and pens a monthly "letter" that is mailed to thousands on his mailing list. A collection of his letters was published in March 2003 in a book called *It's a Terrible Day, Thanks Be to God*. Excerpts from that book, read by Martin Sheen, created the documentary, *The Poet of Poverty*.

MEREDITH GOULD, PH.D. is the author of eight books including, *Deliberate Acts of Kindness: Service as a Spiritual Practice* (Doubleday) and *Why Is There a Menorah on the Altar: Jewish Roots of Christian Worship* (Seabury). In addition to writing about faith, she's a sociologist and digital strategy and communications consultant for churches and mission-based organizations seeking to create and sustain community with online technologies. For more information, please visit: www.meredithgould.com.

REV. PAUL A. HOLMES, S.T.D., a priest of the Archdiocese of Newark since 1981, is Distinguished University Professor of Servant Leadership at Seton Hall University. A native of New Jersey, he graduated Seton Hall with a B.A. in sociology and, in five years of study at the North American College in Rome, Father Holmes earned an S.T.B. *magna cum laude* from the Gregorian University and an S.T.L. *summa cum laude* in moral theology from the Lateran University's Academia Alfonsiana.

While ministering at Newark's Cathedral parish, he received an S.T.M. at Yale University, working with Benedictine liturgist Aidan Kavanagh. He also earned a doctorate *magna cum laude* from Rome's University of St. Thomas Aquinas ('Angelicum'). In 1992, Father Holmes helped inaugurate *Clergy Consultation and Treatment Service*, an interdisciplinary outpatient treatment program for priests at St. Vincent's Hospital in Westchester, New York, and has recently returned to serve once again as the program's Spiritual Director.

Father Holmes was invited to be the first occupant of the Carl J. Peter Chair of Preaching at the North American College while on sabbatical (1999-2000). Returning to Seton Hall, he was named Associate Provost for Academic Administration, continuing to teach courses in moral and sacramental theology. As the University's first Vice President for Mission and Ministry, he led the efforts to obtain a $2-million award from Lilly Endowment, establishing the Center for Vocation and Servant

Leadership. He then served as Vice President and Interim Dean of the Whitehead School of Diplomacy and International Relations and, later, as the University's Executive Vice President.

Father Holmes has published articles in numerous journals and was invited to create *This Sunday's Scripture*, the first homily service of Twenty-Third Publications. He has also offered a number of "Authentic Preaching" practicums to seminarians, deacons and priests from around the English-speaking world. In collaboration with the National Leadership Roundtable on Church Management, he has developed the Toolbox for Pastoral Management, offered twice a year, teaching new pastors the administrative skills needed to lead a vibrant Catholic parish in the 21st century.

DEACON GREG KANDRA is the Executive Editor of *ONE*, the award-winning magazine published by Catholic Near East Welfare Association (CNEWA), a pontifical society founded by Pope Pius XI in 1926. He is also the author of the popular blog, "The Deacon's Bench," carried on the spiritual website, Patheos. Named "One of the Top 10 Catholic Blogs" by religion writer David Gibson, "The Bench" has attracted over four million visitors from around the world since it was launched in 2007, and today garners over 200,000 page views a month.

Before joining CNEWA, Deacon Greg spent nearly three decades in broadcast journalism, most of that time at CBS News, where he was a writer and producer for a variety of programs including *48 Hours, 60 Minutes II, Sunday Morning* and *The CBS Evening News with Katie Couric*. He was also the founding editor of "Couric & Co.," Katie Couric's blog at CBSNews.com.

In 2002, he co-wrote the acclaimed CBS documentary *9/11*, hosted by Robert DeNiro, which told the story of firefighters on September 11, 2001. The film showed the only footage shot inside the World Trade Center that day, and featured the last images of Fr. Mychal Judge, moments before he became the first official fatality of the attacks.

Deacon Greg has received every major award in broadcasting—including two Emmys, two Peabody Awards and four awards from the Writer's Guild of America. He has been honored twice by the Catholic Press Association. He also serves as a consultant to the Communications Committee of the USCCB.

He and his wife live in Forest Hills, New York, where he serves as deacon at Our Lady Queen of Martyrs parish. You can follow Deacon Greg on his blog at: http://www.patheos.com/blogs/deaconsbench/

DEACON JIM KNIPPER is a Roman Catholic deacon serving the Diocese of Trenton, N.J. When not serving his faith community at St. Paul's in Princeton he is CEO of J. Knipper and Company, Inc., which provides a variety of services to the healthcare industry.

In 1981, Jim graduated from the University of Scranton with a degree in Chemistry and in 1984 he received a Master's in Business in the Pharmaceutical Industry from Fairleigh Dickinson University. He is currently pursuing his Masters in Theology from Georgian Court University.

He is a member of the Board of Trustees for Georgian Court University, the only Catholic University in the Trenton Diocese, and a member of the Board of Trustees for the University of Scranton – one of the 28 Jesuit colleges and universities in the United States. Jim is also a Trustee at the Basilica of the National Shrine of the Immaculate Conception in Washington, D.C.

Deacon Jim lives with his wife, Teresa, in Princeton and Cape May, NJ and is father of four sons.

You can follow him on his blog site: http://teachbelief.blogspot.com and on his Facebook page: www.facebook.com/teachbelief

MICHAEL LEACH is publisher emeritus and editor-at-large of Orbis Books. A leader in Catholic publishing for more than 30 years, he has edited and published more than two thousand books. His authors include Nobel Prize winners, National Book Award winners, and hundreds of Catholic Book Award winners. He has served as president of the Catholic Book Publishers Association and the ecumenical Religion Publishers Group. Before joining Orbis as director and publisher in 1997 Michael was president of the Crossroad/Continuum Publishing Group in New York City. In 2007 the Catholic Book Publishers Association honored him with a Lifetime Achievement Award. Dubbed "the dean of Catholic book publishing" by *U.S. Catholic* magazine, he has also authored or edited several books of his own, including the bestsellers *Why Stay Catholic?* and *I Like Being Catholic, A Maryknoll Book of Prayer, The People's Catechism*, and *I Like Being Married*. A popular speaker at Catholic conferences nationwide, Mike lives in Connecticut with his wife of forty-two years Vickie.

FR. RICHARD G. MALLOY, S.J., aka "Mugs," was born at Temple University Hospital in Philadelphia, and earned a doctorate at in Cultural Anthropology from Temple (He didn't go very far in life!) His dissertation was an ethnographic study of Puerto Rican leaders in Camden, NJ.

After being educated by the Sisters of Mercy in grade school he went on to the Jesuit high school in Philadelphia, St. Joseph's Prep. He attended Lafayette College in Easton, PA, and then entered the Jesuit Novitiate in Wernersville, PA. While in Jesuit formation, he spent two years teaching High School in Osorno, Chile and one year in Pastoral work in Santiago.

For 15 years (1988-2003), Fr. Malloy lived and worked at Holy Name Church in Camden, NJ, as a member of the Jesuit Urban Service Team (JUST). From 1994-2008 he also taught at St. Joseph's University in Philadelphia. Fr. Malloy is the author of *A Faith That Frees: Catholic Matters for the 21st Century* (Orbis 2008). The book won an award from The Catholic Press Association in the "Best Presentation of the Faith" category. From 2008 to 2010, Fr. Malloy served at the Sisters of St. Joseph's Chestnut Hill College in Philadelphia. He taught cultural anthropology, directed the intercultural foundations program, and served as a chaplain to the college community.

In September 2010, he was sent to the University of Scranton where he serves as the Vice President of Mission and Ministry, working with campus ministry, community outreach, service learning and international service trips. He teaches cultural anthropology, lives in a freshman dorm (anthropological fieldwork!) and plays his guitar to awaken students who fall asleep in class or during his homilies.

Fishing is his passion in life, and he prays for the day when he will catch a 10 lb. trout or a 47 inch Muskie. He is convinced that such a catch, the Eagles winning the Super Bowl, or the Phillies beating the Yankees in the World Series, are all sure signs that the second coming of Jesus is at hand.

You can follow Fr. Malloy on his blog: http://jesuitjottings.blogspot.com/

FR. JAMES MARTIN, S.J., is a Jesuit priest, author, and contributing editor of *America*, the national Catholic magazine. Father Martin is the author of several books, including *The Jesuit Guide to (Almost) Everything*, which was a *New York Times* bestseller and won a Christopher Award in 2010. His memoir *My Life with the Saints*, which also received a Christopher Award, and his book *Between Heaven and Mirth: Why Joy, Humor and Laughter are at the Heart of the Spiritual Life*, were both named

"Best Books of the Year" by *Publishers Weekly*. His books have been translated into Spanish, German, Chinese, Portuguese, Korean, Polish, Lithuanian and Slovenian.

Father Martin entered the Jesuits in 1988, after graduating from The Wharton School of Business and working at General Electric for six years. During his Jesuit training, he worked in a homeless shelter and with the seriously ill in Boston; at a hospice run by the Missionaries of Charity in Kingston, Jamaica; with street-gang members, and with the unemployed, in Chicago; as a prison chaplain in Boston; and, for two years, in Nairobi, Kenya, with the Jesuit Refugee Service, where he helped East African refugees start small businesses. He received his Master's Degree in Divinity (M.Div.) and in Theology (Th.M.) from the Weston Jesuit School of Theology in Cambridge, Mass. and was ordained a priest in 1999. Since his ordination he has received honorary degrees from several colleges and universities.

Father Martin has written for a variety of publications, both religious and secular, including *The New York Times*, *The Wall Street Journal*, *The Boston Globe*, *Slate* and *The Huffington Post*, and has appeared on all the major networks, including venues as diverse as CNN, BBC, the History Channel and Vatican Radio. He has also been featured on such programs as NPR's "Fresh Air with Terry Gross," PBS's "Newshour," Fox-TV's "The O'Reilly Factor," and Comedy Central's "The Colbert Report." Father Martin blogs regularly for *America* magazine's "In All Things," posts to a public Facebook page (www.facebook.com/FrJamesMartin) and Tweets under @JamesMartinSJ.

BROTHER MICKEY O'NEILL MCGRATH, an Oblate of St. Francis de Sales, is an artist and author of eleven books. The most recent one, published by WLP in 2012 is *Saved by Beauty*, a visual and spiritual journey with Dorothy Day. In addition, his paintings are commissioned by parishes and schools around the country.

Bro. Mickey is a popular presenter and keynote speaker at conferences, parishes, and retreat centers throughout the United States (and Canada), speaking on the connections between art and religious faith. Mickey has created art for many of today's leading Catholic publishers. Since 1987 he has been a summer faculty member of the Grunewald Guild in Leavenworth, Washington where he has been officially designated a "Guild Master."

In 2010, Mickey enjoyed two memorable events: His painting, *Christ the Teacher*, was presented to Pope Benedict XVI; and *St. Cecilia's Orchestra*, (World Library Publications), a collaboration with Alan Hommerding, was awarded a silver medal for children's books on spirituality by the Moonbeam Children's Book Publisher awards.

In 2008, Mickey was the recipient of the THEA BOWMAN Black Catholic Education Foundation Award, in recognition of his work on behalf of Sr. Thea Bowman, his great hero and inspiration. He was blessed to visit her home in Canton, MS in 2010.

Bro. Mickey currently lives and works in Camden, NJ. You can visit his website at www.beestill.org

REV. CAROL HOWARD MERRITT grew up along the beaches of Florida. After being raised as a conservative Baptist and attending a fundamentalist Bible college, she went to Austin Presbyterian Theological Seminary and decided to become a minister. Carol has been a pastor for 13 years, serving growing Presbyterian Churches in the swamps of Cajun Louisiana, a bayside village in Rhode Island, and in an urban neighborhood in D.C. She is the award-winning author of *Tribal Church* (Alban 2007) and *Reframing Hope* (Alban 2010). She has contributed to numerous books, websites, magazines, and journals. Her blog, *TribalChurch.org*, is hosted by the Christian Century. She blogs regularly at *Huffington Post*, Augsburg Fortress's *The Hardest Question*, and Dukes Divinity's *Faith* and *Leadership* sites. Carol is a sought-after speaker.

She hosts *Unco* (short for Unconference), open-space gatherings where participants dream about and plan for the future of the church. She co-hosts *God Complex Radio*, a podcast with Derrick Weston. Carol lives in Chattanooga, TN with her daughter and husband, Brian Merritt, who is starting a new church. You can follow her on Twitter (@CarolHoward) or on Facebook (www.facebook.com/carolhowardmerritt).

REVEREND PENNY A. NASH serves as Associate Rector for Youth, Children, and Families at Bruton Parish Episcopal Church in Williamsburg, Virginia. She was ordained in 2008 in the Episcopal Diocese of Atlanta after receiving her priestly formation and M.Div. (with a Certificate in Anglican Studies) from the Candler School of Theology at Emory University. She served several parishes in the Atlanta area before her call to Bruton where, in addition to "family ministry," she is also engaged in young adult ministry at both the parish and diocesan level.

She loves working in "downtown Colonial Williamsburg," where she parks next to a horse and serves communion to people who come to the altar rail in 18th century costume. An avid fan and user of social media, she assisted fellow-author Meredith Gould in launching the *#chsocm* (Church Social Media) blog (www.churchsocmed. blogspot.com) and weekly Tweetchats and has led Diocesan workshops on the use of social media for ministry and to build connection and community.

She has written meditations for Forward Movement publications as well as serving as a "celebrity blogger" in the annual Lent Madness online devotional (www.lentmadness.org). An amateur photographer, she posts daily prayers, reflections, and visual meditations (*i.e.*, her photos) at *One Cannot Have Too Large a Party* (www.penelopepiscopal.blogspot.com). Follow her on Twitter (www.twitter.com/penelopepiscopl), FourSquare (www.foursquare.com/penelopepiscopl) or friend her on Facebook (www.facebook.com/penny.nash.733).

MSGR. WALTER E. NOLAN is a retired Catholic priest within the Diocese of Trenton, N.J. He received a BS degree in Pharmacy from Fordham University, a Masters Degree in Divinity from Pope John University in Massachusetts, and a Masters Degree in Pastoral Counseling from Iona College. He served as Associate Pastor of St. Gregory's; Chaplain and Athletic Moderator of Notre Dame High School; Chaplain at Rider University; Director of Priest's Personnel for the Diocese and served the Catholic community of Princeton as pastor of St. Paul Church for fourteen years before retirement. He continues to host the Trenton Diocese Catholic Corner radio and TV show.

FR. RICHARD ROHR OFM is a globally recognized ecumenical teacher bearing witness to the universal awakening within mystical and transformational traditions. A Franciscan priest of the New Mexico Province, and founder of the Center for Action and Contemplation (CAC) in Albuquerque, New Mexico, home of the Rohr Institute, his teaching is grounded in practices of contemplation and lived *kenosis* (self-emptying), expressing itself in radical compassion, particularly for the socially marginalized.

Fr. Richard is the author of numerous books, including *The Naked Now*, *Everything Belongs*, *Adam's Return*, *Breathing Under Water*, *Falling Upward*, and *Immortal Diamond: The Meaning of Resurrection and the Search for True Self*.

CAC is home to The Rohr Institute and its Living School for Action and Contemplation. Fr. Richard is available to speak to groups convening in the New Mexico area. To learn more about the school visit www.cac.org. You can also follow him on:

Facebook: www.facebook.com/CenterforActionandContemplation
Twitter: @RichardRohrOFM

FRAN ROSSI SZPYLCZYN is a writer with a focus on how spirituality intersects with daily life. A former senior corporate executive in the media business, she is now the Office Manager at the Church of the Immaculate Conception in Glenville, NY. Fran worships at St. Edward the Confessor in Clifton Park, NY, where she is involved in liturgical ministry and catechesis. As a student at St. Bernard's School of Theology and Ministry, Fran is working towards an MA in Pastoral Studies. Her work has been published in *The Evangelist*, the newspaper of the Roman Catholic Diocese of Albany, in the *Albany Times Union* and in the *National Catholic Reporter*. She lives in Clifton Park, NY with her husband Mark and her stepdaughter Erica. You can explore her work at her personal blog, *There Will Be Bread*. (http://blog.timesunion.com/bread) Fran also hosts blogs for her two parishes, which can be found at *The Parish Blog of St. Edward the Confessor* (http://stedwardsblog.wordpress.com) and *Pastoral Postings* (http://pastoralpostings.wordpress.com) Follow Fran on Twitter @FranSzpylczyn and on Facebook at www.facebook.com/fran.szpylczyn.

Continue to follow our work

and stay connected with us at:

www.facebook.com/Homilists

THE CHARITIES

CRANALEITH SPIRITUAL CENTER is a ministry of the Sisters of Mercy that offers a safe space of hospitality, beauty, and peace to all who seek to know their home in the heart of God where each one's dignity and promise can flourish. This "sanctuary of trees" welcomes people of all walks of life to wholeness and transformation for themselves and for society. Here, friends from the homeless community and suburban neighbors feast together on the garden's harvest they tend with one another. Here, all are rich, and all find themselves poor, but for one another. Cranaleith's programs sustain the healing of those recovering from life's traumas, support groups and individuals who wish to renew their spirit for life and work, and extend opportunities for guests to reflect on what matters deeply in their lives. Dedicated in a special way to those who are poor, Cranaleith welcomes those at the center of need and those at the center of influence to reflection, dialogue and meaningful partnerships.

For more information please visit us online at http://www.cranaleith.org/ or on Facebook at www.facebook.com/pages/Cranaleith-Spiritual-Center/209033702468528

For thirty years **SEVERAL SOURCES SHELTERS** has focused on saving babies' lives and sheltering their young mothers while providing education and ongoing compassionate support services and teaching Holy Chastity. They educate young people to make healthy life choices and shelter women who are homeless, sick, and elderly and help them to restore their dignity. Through God's grace, Several Sources Shelters save babies' lives and shelter their young mothers while providing education and ongoing compassionate support services. We further educate young people to make healthy life choices.

Over 20,000 babies have been saved through the efforts of the Several Sources Shelters since Founder Kathy DiFiore took into her own home her first pregnant teenager in 1981. Kathy says that Several Sources Shelters started with the Prayer of St. Francis of Assisi: "Make me a channel of Your Peace. Where there is darkness, let me sow light. Where there is sadness, let me bring joy."

Their most recent project includes a mobile sonogram which provides free sonograms to pregnant women outside abortion clinics in New Jersey.

For more information, please visit us online at http://www.severalsourcesfd.org/

The **TRENTON AREA SOUP KITCHEN** (TASK) was founded by a small group of individuals from local churches and service organizations. Their goal was to feed the truly needy people of Trenton five days a week.

On a cold day in January of 1982, sixty hungry people gathered for TASK's first meal in the basement of a Trenton church. By the end of that year, more than 40,000 meals had been served. No one knew there were so many hungry people in Trenton.

Through the generosity of area foundations, corporations, civic groups, community organizations, labor unions, churches, synagogues, and more than 2,500 individuals, enough money was raised to build our current facility on land made available by the City of Trenton at 72 ½ Escher Street. In July 1991, the first meal was served in the new facility.

Today, TASK's mission is to feed those who are hungry in the Trenton area and offer programs to encourage self-sufficiency and improve the quality of life of its patrons. In 2012, over 195,000 meals were served. To meet the growing need, TASK has partnered with churches and social service organizations to create satellite meal service locations in South Trenton, West Trenton, Hightstown, and Princeton. TASK programs have also expanded to include adult education, computer training, health care counseling, screening and referrals, social services, a performing arts/music/creative writing program, a visual arts program, and special programs for children.

TASK patrons are unemployed, underemployed, or do not earn a living wage. Many of the people served have addictions, mental illnesses or physical health problems that make it difficult to obtain or maintain a job. Others have little or no education and very low self-esteem, which makes it nearly impossible for one to even begin to overcome obstacles to self-sufficiency. In the past few years, TASK has seen an increase in the number of recent immigrants using its services. Illegal status and language are barriers for many of these individuals.

TASK serves approximately 3,750 meals each week. Those who come to TASK include the elderly, the addicted, the mentally ill, the physically challenged, veterans, recent immigrants, families with children, the working poor, and the newly unemployed. Since its inception, TASK has had an open-door, no-questions-asked policy. Service is unconditional, and everyone who comes is served.

Volunteers are the backbone of TASK. The staff is small, but is able to accomplish much with the help of the individuals and groups who generously give their time. For more information about TASK please visit our website at www.trentonsoupkitchen.org or on our Facebook page at https://www.facebook.com/TrentonAreaSoupKitchen

WOMANSPACE, INC., founded in 1977, is a leading nonprofit agency in Mercer County, New Jersey, that provides a comprehensive array of services to individuals and families impacted by domestic and sexual violence and dedicated to improving the quality of life for women and their families. Our bilingual (English and Spanish) programs include 24-hour crisis intervention through crisis hotlines, response teams, and emergency shelter, counseling for adults and children, court advocacy, and housing services. Our goal is to assist survivors both at the moment of crisis and throughout their journey of emotional healing and the achievement of economic independence.

Womanspace is one of only eight agencies in the state that is specifically focused on providing potentially life-saving services to victims and survivors of domestic violence, sexual assault, dating violence, stalking, and human trafficking. Domestic violence and sexual assault are not just women's issues, and they are not just individual or family problems. Violence against women is a human issue and a social problem. It's up to the community to take a stand against abuse, hold abusers accountable for their behavior, and protect victims. No victim of domestic violence or sexual assault is turned away due to an inability to pay.

Womanspace affirms its commitment to cultural competency. We recognize and value the ethnic, religious, and racial richness of our communities, and encourage mutual respect and understanding among all people. True excellence in our organization and communities results from identifying, serving, and enlisting the participation of all people who represent this rich diversity.

Womanspace is a 501(c)(3) tax-exempt organization and receives funding from the State of New Jersey, the County of Mercer, and contributions from individuals, organizations, foundations, and corporations. If you or someone you know is a victim of domestic or sexual violence and needs help, please call our 24-hour hotline at (609) 394-9000.

For more information about Womanspace please visit us online at www.womanspace.org or on our Facebook page at https://www.facebook.com/pages/Womanspace-Inc/151692311521382

ACKNOWLEDGEMENTS

Taking a raw concept and idea and bringing it to full fruition takes a talented and dedicated team. And, indeed, I am blessed with so many friends and professionals who worked with me to give birth to this book!

My thanks and blessings to…

… Joelle Chase, whose keen eye added great value to the content.

… Dave Clarfield, who was instrumental in dotting the i's and crossing the t's.

… Steve Clarfield, who opened my eyes 25 years ago to the P's, K's, M's and C's of life. That, along with his friendship, has made all the difference in my life.

… Doug Cordes, who gave style and design to my concept.

… Meredith Gould, who has been an ever guiding light for so many years and who encouraged and supported me from the very first thought of this book.

… Mike Krupa, whose flawless print production pulled it all together.

… Mickey McGrath, whose incredible artwork blesses the words that have been printed.

… Maureen, Linda, Nancy, Joanne, Mike, Frank, Joe, and all the employees at J. Knipper and Company who support me with time and space to work on my passion.

… Tim, Jon, Peter and Jacob Knipper, my sons, who provide me much joy and love and homiletic stories.

… Teresa, my wife who is truly the love of my life in every way.

… And, of course, to all of the Homilists for the Homeless in the volume, for your "yes" of faith in this project and for your insight, wisdom and graces in breaking open the Gospel to all.